Keep It Moving

Debora Shannon

www.WeAreAPS.com

Table of Contents

FOREWORD

I am very excited about the publication of *Keep it Moving!* Evangelist Shannon has spent in depth time praying and seeking the Lord regarding the content and context of this book. Her desire is for all to come into the knowledge of Christ Jesus and develop a sincere relationship with the one who can give eternal life.

Throughout her text, Evangelist Shannon seeks to address life issues as we learn how to focus on the present situation and not our past. For in our past failures, we can either get stuck on why we did not accomplish our goals, which can keep us bound in bondage. On the other hand, we can look at how God has allowed our circumstances to strengthen us in areas where our dependency was in our own ability opposed to drawing on His strength. The closer our relationship is with the Lord, the more we can see His revealed truths in our lives.

To help readers open their inner most thoughts and secrets to the Father, Evangelist Shannon has provided specific prayers after each chapter that will guide the reader into spiritual fellowship and worship. It is time to release our disappointments and adopt the spirit of overcoming! Now is the time to understand why the enemy wanted you to remain blind and never come into the purpose and fulfillment God has on your life! Jesus has already forgiven you. His love will cover you, and His Spirit will guide you as you learn to trust Him.

Keep it Moving will help motivate, encourage, and provide you with tools and resources to navigate life and combat the tricks of the enemy. Allow the leading of this God-fearing woman of God lead you to a greater hope in Christ Jesus!

Blessings,

Pastor, Dr. Yolanda Cosey

CHAPTER 1

Lying Dormant

What is lying dormant in your life? Is there something hidden you refuse to face? Something hidden that you do not want anyone to know? I have things lying dormant in my life. Somethings I am just now learning to face. Other things I am learning to deal with as I go along. Things I just have to grow through. I'm forced to look at the situation that was designed to take me out. No more pretending; it is what it is and I am prepared now to make those adjustments. I am putting on my "big girl undies" and I am going to move forward. I'm moving pass the past. Some things I have no control over, but those things I can change, I am going to deal with, once and for all. I am who I am, and I am learning to love who God made me to be. What a nice place to be in.

Vanity

Don't get me wrong, I still wear wigs, and makeup, which was once frowned upon in some of the churches, but now seems to be acceptable. I am, a rules and regulations type of girl, but every now and then I will break the norm, not to be defiant, but to remind myself I am not a robot. I don't think God wants our praise and worship to be robotic; He wants true worship. So, my goal is to worship and draw nigh to Him with a pure heart.

I will never forget one Sunday I had my wig cap on, dressed and almost out the door, until I looked in the mirror. It was funny, and child I would have been embarrassed, maybe? I said all that because God is more concerned about our hearts than our appearances. Case in point, the bible talks about two brothers who promised their father two different things. One said, Father I will not go, and the other said, I will go. Did these brothers have something lying dormant within them, and did one respond as a robot, and the other from the heart?

Now these hidden areas, what are they? Let's approach the negative first, and then we will take it to a very positive place, by recognizing all the spiritual things that are given the children of God. Things meant for the body of Christ to use for the building of His kingdom. These gifts are lying dormant inside of us, too.

Lying dormant inside of us, are hidden areas that we cover up or hide from others, and many times, those hidden dark areas come out without us knowing or understanding why. Intentionally or unintentionally, sometimes we display the signs and symptoms of those things lying dormant. How many lessons have you learned by observing another person? How relaxed or uncomfortable did they appear? Withdrawn or outgoing? Easy to get along with, or unwilling to cooperate in group settings?

Jesus helps us with this issue of seeing the faults of others. Sometimes, we can see others and their hidden fears and judge them right or wrong, but the Lord said, "Remove the beam in your own eye before taking the mote out of thy brother's eye." (Matthew 7:5, KJV). Before I can help others, I need to check my own issues. When we are honest with ourselves, we have a better chance of receiving God's help for pulling out of us what was meant to be seen, heard, and known of men. Not that stuff we are ashamed about, and don't know what to do with, but the way God meant for us to address our place in the world, the place where we make a difference.

Last point, when Jesus had finished his forty day fast, He was tempted of the devil; once the three main temptations were successfully rejected by our Lord, the devil went away for a season. We learned from this incident that there are three main enemies of our souls: the lust of the flesh (what the body wants); the lust of the eye (what our minds have imagined); and the pride of life (being boastful about our accomplishments and material possessions).

This chapter will help us to affirm our commitment to ourselves, and tackle the hidden area(s) of our lives that currently need attention. We can now become alive to those things that matter. Things that are right and good for us. We can melt away those habits that may harm us, like matters that are not in our best interest. We can purge ourselves of those extra pains and hurts, which are lying dormant inside of us, waiting to jaunt us up or cause us to echo the same offenses against our God, ourselves, and others.

My first book explained my interest in going to the cross frequently, and in this book, I extend an invitation for you to come too. You can do this at home, or every Sunday while singing, ushering or sitting in the pews, or in the pulpit. You can go to the cross while on your security post, or riding the bus. Learn who Christ is, and how to become a saint, refuting disobedience, and standing up for righteousness.

We may always have sin tendencies, but we don't have to sin, or practice sin. We have a gatekeeper, an advocate in Christ Jesus. I encourage you to do as 1 Peter 5:7 advises, "Cast your cares on him. for he cares for you." While you are on your job, at home alone, you can get answers, and press forward and be contented. I believe in order to find contentment we must learn to love, like, and show concern for the person God has called us to be.

The core part of you is waiting for the manifestation of God's covering for your life. Your soul knows right well who Jesus is. Allow God to have the preeminence in your life. Let him in through Christ Jesus. You will enjoy the illumination and the freedom that comes with salvation. You will have a new compass, a new course to take, an enjoyable journey, even through the difficult times.

We were created in His image and in His likeness, and He made so much beauty in the world that we must fight very hard not to notice it. Some things interfere with that splendor, such as when people take us for granted or we take our blessings for granted; perhaps just not being aware of how significant we are to God and how much He cares for us. If you have come to grips with your own mortality then you are ready to make that lasting change. The change that will last throughout infinity. Come with me to the cross, you will never be the same again.

If you have read my first book, you know that Mr. Jackson, was a good dad, and he always had an answer for my biblical questions. I never felt uncomfortable around my dad; I trusted him then, and I trust him now. I would ask Dad all kinds of questions about God, and he always had a good answer for me. He made it difficult for me to keep things dormant. I was always trying to clean the little dirty things I knew were inside of me, like jealousy, anger or wanting my way all the time – not to mention being selfish with my worldly possessions. I wanted my own bedroom. I didn't want to share with my brothers, not even let them watch television in my room. I didn't realize how important it was to have those special moments. Moments you will need later in life.

One special moment I will not forget is when my mom bought me my first hygienic kit in 1965; I was 10 years old. It was pink and had all kinds of girl things inside to help one, to get use to becoming a young lady. I held on to that kit, and looked at it ever so often. You might say that it was lying dormant. I am not sure if they have those kinds of things today, but I thank God for the booklets that explained how I was going to feel once my period started. And I must admit if my mother had not given me that particular gift, I would have been frightened to the changes that were going to take place in my body.

I took the pink box to my grandmother's house the following year when she took me in to live with her and Frank (granddad). My period didn't start until I was twelve. I explained the symptoms to my grandmother; she was not able to help me. She didn't understand that I was transitioning into womanhood, or as they would say back then, experiencing the "change". Other than that, Grandmother was my best friend; she was a super mom, to me, sacrificing her own independence.

I could talk to her about anything. She made me feel loved and accepted, important and smart. No one ever knew she was my grandmother, because she never drew attention to herself, even when I sang in church. She didn't make me feel important in public, but she did, when I spent hours at her feet, rubbing them listening to the stories of her life. She taught me how I should handle certain situations that may arise in my life. Was she street smart or saintly? It was the former; but more than being street, she loved me and I adored her. I had a good grandmother.

Now that I am a mother and grandmother, I realize, that she really wanted the best for me. She is long gone from this earth, yet she lives within me. She could probably see the days ahead, and knew that I would be independent. Far from the life she was used to seeing in her friends and even in some places of her own life. She is in my heart forever; I used to miss her, but now I feel she is somehow near as I live and learn. By this I mean a principal of motherly love.

Never to forget, my mom sacrificed too. She carried me and ushered me into this world, and no matter how Grandmother loved and carried me and prepared me for life, Mom didn't abort me. She carried me nine months. Thank you, Mom. I am so sorry that we both have wasted so much time wanting each other's love, and not knowing how to make that happen without clashing. We too shall overcome someday.

She is older now, and some of the things that kept us apart are merely forgotten. I try harder to love and please her in some small way because I realize she loves me in her own way. I remember when I turned thirteen, my mother bought a home on 104th and Green Street, in Chicago, and my grandparents and I moved there with mom and Robert Jr. I had to go to the cross a lot after I got saved because it was hard coming from a broken home, always feeling like something was missing. This little fox of forgiveness, was lying dormant. But I was not able to fix it, even thou I raised my children with their dad. I couldn't go back and since he left me, I was part of a broken home once again.

My objective is now resting in the fact that I am from a royal family and God has given me a new home with them that our sanctified, which includes my mom. I remember sharing the gospel with her on several occasions; one Sunday night I got through to her, and that following Friday she got baptized and came up speaking in tongues.

By the time I was fifteen I was with my brother and mother, and felt unstable living without my grandmother. What was lying dormant inside of me? I thought my mom should have stayed with my dad, but she divorced him. Then she flared up at my grandmother and asked her to leave. I call my mom by her first name (Darlene) whenever I need to keep my head straight to avoid getting caught up in drama from the past. Darlene did to my dad what my ex did to me. But God is asking for me (and those of you who may have a similar story) to get over it and "keep it moving."

As much as I loved my mom, I didn't trust her. What was lying dormant in me, was the fact that she liked me some days and some days she didn't. I missed the structure that my grandmother supplied, but she and granddaddy Frank moved into their own home, near Fenger High School, on 112th and Wallace Avenue, which was a nice long walk from mom's house on Green Street.

Mom was pretty connected to Chicago's bosses (political friends); some got in trouble, and some lived nice long lives. So even though she may have appeared to have it all together, something happened. I was too young to know how bad it was for her and was soon back with my grandmother. Mom was missing from my life after that for a space of three years, when I ran away. I didn't want to be like her and drop out of school, so I ran away, because I had no intentions of being a nobody. I was not going to let her boyfriend have his way with me. But Robert Jr. loved her without question. He was her guardian angel.

I never mentioned to my grandmother's play-daughter Ruby, who was like a daughter. She looked just like my grandmother; she loved her as if that was her true mother. I guess she really was kind of like the way I feel about Georgia, my dad's wife (of about 50 years now). Although she is a retired school teacher, she still uses the opportunity to teach. encouraging her own son, and her stepchildren.

I will never forget when Georgia brought me my first typewriter. My mother was jealous about that, and bought me a new one a little later; I appreciated both typewriters. I was typing about 65 words a minute; typing was my stress reliever. It certainly comes in handy to have this skill, which is something I still find very useful when I am writing reports for my present job. I consider it priceless.

Christopher and Larry were the first bullies in my life. I had to find a way to rid myself of them, and I did that without having to tell my parents. Although I was afraid of them, I wouldn't let them know. It hurt really bad, when they would trip me in the cold winter. On 78th and Green, across the street from Oglesby School, it was the winter of 1963...I'll never forget. I guess you can say, thanks to those two guys, I am not afraid of bullies, although the rest of the bullies in my life were minimal. Bullies were on the job, at the grocery store, and yes, at church (not my present church). God has strengthened me to be more than a conquer because of my Lord and Savior Jesus Christ.

Sexual Immorality

What is lying dormant? He is married but he didn't tell you. You are married and he knows it. Back out of that hole you're in and grasp the word of God. Look up every scripture on marriage, adultery and fornication. God, wash us from every evil work. Continue to bless every single woman and man to abstain, and to please you. In Jesus' name.

Will God deliver you? Yes. He has all power, and He will deliver you out of every evil work. For no weapon that is meant to destroy you will prosper; cling to God, watch Him, He will work on your behalf. I am not giving you a "go ahead and do it" card, but I am saying tell God you want help, and watch Him strengthen you away from those things that are not pleasing to Him, and that tax you. I can promise you that you will notice the change in your life, and God will remove all uncleanliness from your life day-by-day, month-by-month, year-by-year. Be healed, be delivered, be set free. Hallelujah! Be aroused by your spouse alone. Be aroused by the word of God... tell yourself to think on the things of Christ. The things that are pure, of virtue, honest and of a Good report. (KJV) Philippians 4:8

"God's got a way that's mighty sweet..." the old saint would sing that song. I lay my burden down at his feet. He keeps my soul, from day to day. God's got a way that's mighty sweet.

Back in the day, during the late 60' and early 80's, ministers didn't want saved people to let their children play with unsaved children. They didn't want their kids going to the movie theaters or having a television in the house. Today, technology is the way of the world. We may not want to give them credit, but for sure they would certainly call the phone the same... or some "uncircumcised gadge", not to mention the mighty "Facebook series".

I am not trying to kick against the times, but we must be grateful for the old time way, and recognize (as I heard a preacher say on television) that the Bible is the book for all times; it never changes or goes out of style. So, following the rules and regulations of God's command, is going to bring life to each generation. Can you see why God made man and woman to be joined as one? God made sex, and He made it for the two, man and woman to become one. (to bare good fruit). To populate the world with His original plan.

Lord, give me the strength I need to by-pass the natural part of the flesh, to deny it, in order to please You.

The Bible is the word of God, and it is "God breathed." What does that mean? It is inspired and protected by the Holy One, just as God gave Moses the commandments. The word of God is the same yesterday, today and forevermore. It is a constant. The constant that never changes. (God is the same), God said; and it was. It is, and it shall be.

Thus, saith the Lord, stand ye in the ways and see, ask for the old paths, where is the good way and walk therein, and ye shall find rest for your souls. But they said, we will not walk therein.

This verse is saying: "We will not walk therein". We, here represents a world and a humanistic view. But God is speaking, telling us in order to stay away from a fast-track style ask for the old-time way. The old way tells us to do it God's way. What is the incentive? Rest. The prize is, rest for our souls. Our loving Father has "a way that's mighty sweet". Marriage is honorable in all and the bed undefiled: but whoremongers and adulterers God will judge. With the old way, men honored their wives and stayed with their wives and didn't bring their secret worlds to their door step. Today, men and women are dishonoring Gods law of marriage but it's not too late to remember that it's until death – not until one decides they want to try someone else. I am not angry or bitter because I am no longer married; if I was, I am sure I would still consider this point of view. It's God's plan that this is a holy thing; exclusive for one another; not to be shared. It is sacred and God ordained and blessed the union. It should not be interfered with.

One may ask me the question, and I will answer you. Why not take your ex-husband back? The scripture gives me grounds and I am standing by my decision not to go back; the fear is prudent. The fear is that he may not be persuaded to be stable till death, and when I asked the Holy Ghost about this matter August of 2011, the words came to me, "If you can stand the pain you feel right now then take him back." (as of summer 2018) Willie remarried in his hometown to another, it is my prayer he and she as one will be happy till death, I bless their union.

But as I said in the first book, I can't even imagine being married to him, not because the memories are faded, but because they are faded when it comes to ever being intimate. I believe because he was so brutally cruel with the way he left, and allowed that same behavior to dominate the way he treated me, it made it easier to accept his decision to walk away from his marriage of 32 years. He left a few months before the 31st year, and the divorce was final 1 day after the 32nd year. The pain was so overwhelming at that time, I could not consider ever going back.

But I can and will be kind to him, if he is hungry, I shall feed him; outdoors, I will take him in. If he were sick, I would tend to him; but as a friend and father of my children, as my brother, but never ever as a lover ever again. Please recognize that I am for God's way, but I could not make him stay, and I could not make him cherish me, nor see me as a good wife. He abandoned me, and I am okay with that fact.

I could not keep him in the light, when he was groping after the darkness. I could not make him stay or reason with him, when he did this thing so secretly, so harmful. This thing is unheard of in the Christian faith, and yet more now than should be. It was a nightmare to live through, asking if he could come back is like a dog, returning to rain yellow on the tree he once before rained under. I don't mind being mistreated, but I believe it's important for me to look out for myself. "It's getting late in the evening and the sun is going down." I am a hen, not a chicken. I don't see marriage in my future, but if God allows a man of God to find me, I will marry, I will make sure there are no books in the bed.

Fornication should not be heard of in our lives and the best way I can describe, staying away from this deadly sin, is to not allow ourselves to be put into a situation that would cause us to be tripped up by the adversary. The book of Acts tells us to abstain from fornication. Let us not allow anyone to pressure us or put us in that quandary. Let us think on things that glorify and edify the Lord. Again, I am not giving a "go ahead and do it" card; I am saying once we dedicate our lives to God, He will supply each and every need, which includes a spouse to meet any need that we have if we ask, according to His will. God shall supply our needs. He promised to keep us. So, let us not be foolish, let us draw nigh to God and expect that we will be found in him busy working out our own soul salvation. The flesh battle is swallowed up in prayer and supplication, and perhaps not looking at explicit love scenes, until you know you can manage through those type of episodes.

And if you are not able to follow this line of thinking again, I invite you to the cross. And here, Christ is willing, ready and able to cleanse you and wash you in His blood. He will make you clean inside, and give you power to live a life free from sin.

It will no longer be your way of life or a practice, inherited by our fallen nature. Allow your mind to be a drum major for righteousness, and you will be righteous not of your works but because of the work of the cross of Christ our Lord. Our power is in God's hands, so you need not fear about messing up. The Holy Ghost is a real keeper!

And Jesus came unto them saying, "All power is given unto me in heaven and in earth. "This reminds me of the song some of us have heard on the Gospel radio stations, "I love God, you don't love God? What's wrong with you?" Let's prepare ourselves to build ourselves up on our most holy faith. The faith in which we were called to repentance. It is that faith that will keep us. You who are not saved, let me encourage you when you wean to your new walk, listen to the voice of the Holy Spirit. He is willing to help you; He will carry you through.

13

The disciples asked Jesus to teach them to pray; Christ prayed deliver us from evil. When Judas betrayed Jesus, it was a necessary evil. Our Lord told Judas to do what he must do, quickly. No weapon formed against you shall prosper, Christ was crucified, buried, and resurrected on the third day according to the scripture. Let us bury those things that are on the negative side and allow the resurrection power of the Holy Ghost to raise us up to a place of victory. Against dead works. No weapon formed against Christ ever prospered, not now, not then, and not ever.

So, now let us come and reason with the Lord. Let me walk with you to the cross, I know He can make it better. "Try Christ". You may ask, how can I try Christ, when He is so Holy and I am so sinful? I live with the 1st Adam, how can I rid myself of him and "try Christ" when He is 2nd Adam? Whereas the first is last. And the last is first, according to the scripture, which the Apostle brings out so well in his epistles to the Romans. Romans chapter 6 and 7. Who shall deliver me from this old wretched man that I am? (KJV)

Now, Isaiah said, "Come let us reason saith the Lord, although your sins be as scarlet, they shall be as white as snow." We cannot cleanse ourselves, but Christ has the power and the blue print to make us His loving own. I desire to navigate through this period and time with Christ in control. The gospel makes sense, and when we go to our Lord in prayer, we will hear Him move on our behalf, no matter what.

Your way is already made. Are you at the cross? Are you at the crossroad of change? Letting go of your old man and pressing forward as Christ builds himself a home in you, one that cannot die after this physical Adam has returned God's breath. The same breath God breathed into Adam and Eve.

How can I make it right with God, by faith in the Son of God?

Once you, and Christ work it out, I am sure He will help you. Say what David said in the Psalms, "My help cometh from the Lord who made the heavens and the earth." Your loving Father is waiting for you to take your case to Jesus, the mighty liberator advocates for us, always. Everything is under His control.

Mahalia Jackson would've told you, "It is God who made the mountains, and that He's bigger than you and I. Somebody bigger than you and I." Ask God for strength in your new life. Will you let me pray with you as I close this part of negativity of things that are sitting dormant in side of us.

Dear Lord:

Give each reader, and those who are reading but standing proxy for someone else, that they know, You can reach their friend; I can hear Helen Baylor singing as we pray. Father, give strength to my brother in or out of faith, to my sister in or out of faith, and each of us who stand proxy for those we invite to the cross. Strengthen them to make the best decision they could ever make in this life, which is to give themselves to Jesus.... In Jesus' name. Amen

The Positive Things

I remember the bookcase that was full of books, when we moved to 79th and Green. (as a child). The white people who were the previous homeowners left them; they were husband and wife. Leaving those books in the bookcases was a world of mystery for me. I should have asked Rev. Jackson, if he remembered what they did for a living. Probably retired. By then, probably moving to Tennessee.

On October 14, 2016, I asked God to forgive me for not being better for Him. I know He will remember that I am made of dust. My spirit is willing, but I am moving in a direction that tells me I am no longer vibrant as I once was. I am growing older, but I also know I need to keep it moving to the best life I can, memories and all, and never give up, never give up on the hope of eternal life in Christ.

Appreciate all the compliments: "You look 45 years old," but I am 61. I feel great, but I have days when I recognize my destiny is to go on from here (I'm on my way home-book one). So, I am writing to share, and to help those who have questions and want some answers that I may have learned along the way. I am writing about a lot of things, and how to get beyond some points of our hurts, and some points of rebuilding our self-esteem, and to get beyond some point of being afraid to talk with our Creator and meet and love Him the way He loves us.

I am not trying to convey that Christ will just throw us away or give up on us. He really does care for each of His human creations. He even cares for the grass that turns so many different colors, even dies, but comes alive in spring. Just as the grass dies and returns to life, so can many who suffer with sickness and disease. Right now, I want to pray for people who are on dialysis. I have a brother Lord who has been saved for a few years, but is on dialysis.

Dearest Father: there are so many people who are currently on dialysis treatment. I don't know a lot about these treatments but as You know, Lord, these treatments are most difficult and takes many hours out of the week for the patients to have their blood cleansed. I thank You for those who take the time to help them, those who may be alone during that process, some who have support, others who have staff to assist them. We also ask for better ways for treatment, and that you allow many to receive kidneys and any miracles for better health. In Jesus' name I pray, Amen.

Grace

I wish that I didn't have to experience seeing, men and women sleeping on the street. But they do, and the only consolation I have is "The poor you will have with you always." (KJV). I wish I didn't have to see young people smoking cigarettes; I stopped at 24 yrs. old, which was when the Lord saved me. My own children have never seen me smoke. I pray for our children to have the power to stop smoking. I remember doing a term paper in junior college on smoking cigarettes. I hope that one day, all those who want to finally stop, will have enough grace to do so. I enjoyed smoking, but I am so glad those days are over. The Lord really took the taste away. I struggled before that happened. I would leave service before getting saved, wanting a cigarette. It was such a distraction but the taste and the high was amazing until the Lord took the taste away, I don't miss that messy cough that goes with it. Finally, a breakthrough.

Once you give your life to Christ and find baptism in the name of Jesus, you will want all the world to know; please don't get discouraged when someone does not believe you. Take baby steps. Find yourself a good bible teaching, preaching church (Apostolic Pentecostal). If you do not get the Holy Ghost immediately, wait and tarry, every time you have a tarrying partner. Be Blessed!

What is lying dormant? The gifts of the spirit. They are waiting to be used. The thought is wonderful! The opposition is unbelief. You must get over the fact of how you used to be and move into the place where God wants you to be. I want to give you some tools that will help you embrace the positive gifts given to the new you, in Christ Jesus! Where

can I locate this treasure?

There may have been books in the library on Christianity, but I don't remember seeing them. I remember that they were all hardcover books and I received great pleasure coming home to find those books in my personal library. Every day I would look at many of the books, looking for a story, a line something to grab hold of. Did I allow the books to mean something? The books are still in my mind, but in a place of creativity. In a place of safety, in a place of pure honesty.

I didn't understand every line and sentence text, but the books were in my heart, and maybe that is why I want to learn, an teach and reach. I want to bless and not curse, help and not hurt. The white couple left their music too. If I remember the music was 331/2. Country style. The Tennessee waltzes stood out the most. Dionne Warrick replaced that recording in my mind to *Face it, girl it's over "I'm just sayin'.* Now, those days are over of *Just a little respect, Turn off the Lights* and *Sexual Healing.*

I found a new place to spend some time, while healing from my friend getting married (from book 1). What place is that? Well, besides going to church, which is my duty, it's Walmart! It's Ashley Stewart. And not much longer from now, it will be on a boat cruise.

I feel like cooking again, instead of eating out. I am on the mend, I have heard from him and seen him, but he's married now, and I prove to love the law of the Lord and refuse to settle. As of March 08, 2017, a lot has taken place. Thanks be to God; I am moving on and doing better each and every day. His story is not for me to tell; what I say about him, I will say it metaphorically so that those who may be impacted by the story will see it as some form of behavior, that could be about any given situation. Let's just say I have never met anyone like him and I call him my friend. He made me laugh and caused me to feel like a woman. But now I want to be God's woman...it takes strength to grow and move on and let go. It's not easy. But if you have faith and courage, and allow yourself to be better, it will happen. He has text and called. I need the opportunity to do the same, and that "you are now married allow me to move on too". This was at the end of January 2017. Once again, I feel empowered. The bible lets us know this faith walk is done in parts, let us let go of what is not good for us, let us do it in parts and in stages. Know that God has not forgotten to help us through every situation.

Find all those positive things that are lying dormant inside of you, and exercise that good girl, boy, woman or man. Love her or him and hug yourself daily. Eat well, feel well and ask God to help you to get to that place. You will find new life. It all starts with the Cross experience. "letting go and letting God."

What was lying dormant? Questions and more questions. Why can't people who hurt you answer them? Perhaps, because they feel it's all about them, and they don't know answers any more than we know ourselves. Let's take those feelings to the cross, shall we?

Father We Pray:

Help us move along in our lives from things that may have hurt us while growing up. Help us recognize that we can be washed as we forgive, and be forgiven from those things standing in the shadows, hoping and desiring to freeze our progress. Give us strength to forgive and to be forgiven. We claim healing from things that lie dormant inside of us. We pray for mother and daughter relationships, and that healing will be our bread. In Jesus' name, Amen.

This Little Prayer

I pray for those issues that lie dormant in our lives, saved and unsaved. Those of us who are learning to navigate through life, knowing that what is in that dark place in our hearts need to see the light of day. Father, you have what we need; let your word wash and cleanse us through the blood of Jesus. For the word, which washes, became flesh. Jesus, wash us and increase our faith. Allow us to rid ourselves of hurts and pain that have harassed and imprisoned us because we could not rid ourselves of the guilt and shame of it all. In Jesus' name we pray, Amen.

I want to pray for those things that lie dormant in the negative realm of our lives, that come to weigh us down and dummy us down, and drain us, and zap our energy away from those things that lie dormant inside of us, on our positive side. Those things that need to surface for the better, for what God intended for us to possess in Him, for our lives to have a sure foundation, of the kind of love He wants to give us, so we can recognize clearly our potential. Let us move away from fear, let us see ourselves the way God intended for us to be, right now. It's ok to cry, it's ok to let it all out. Come with me hold, my hand let's take it to the cross.

Prayer At the Cross

Dearest Dad, Father, and Lord! How holy thou art, and we thank You, now for lending your ear to us, to hear this prayer that many of us are praying. For relief for a breakout, and a shout out of praise and worship for who You are and for those who do not know You, but decided to pick up this book, we ask that You would go into the inner most parts of our brothers' and sisters' lives, and heal them from whatever it is that is lying dormant inside, that they may not yet understand.

We ask that You teach each of us now, to come to the cross. Some who come for the very first time to give You the burdens of their hearts. Heal them from feeling dirty, when someone violated them, and it wasn't their fault, then or now. Those who used their bodies and promised to love them, but in the wrong way. Dear God, please help my brother, and my sister who was led into a world of darkness through pornography, where it seems difficult, and where no one seems to talk about it in their surroundings or play it down as though it is alright, when they themselves would prefer to be rid of the dark sexual pics so that they can do things your blessed way, and not the way of the world. Heal husbands and wives of such a dark place that they may know that what they have together is a turn-on enough and that they just need to feel your presence. For You created sexual pleasure for the marriage bed and the marriage bed alone. I remember those days, and know that it is right and it is good, the way you commanded that order. In Jesus' name, we pray. Amen

CHAPTER 2

Good Morning.

---○---

I awaken with the desire to thank God for allowing me to make it through the night. Usually my nights are free from pain, free from stomach and other issues, except for the usual issues that baby boomers have, our parents called it "Uncle Arthur." I rarely have headaches and try to stay away from unnecessary drama. I'm home bodied, and don't like crowds, unless it's for corporate worship, or I crave to be around people, at a concert or at the theater. I like reading and sleeping, and lounging around the house. I don't like talking on the phone as much as I use too. I love decorating my house, changing the décor, listening to the Moody Bible Institute, at home or while in the car, especially at the beginning of the year, because Moody radio gives money tips, such as investments, savings plans and how to prepare an emergency fund. (The Money Talk)

I love winter sleep, because it seems to give your body a chance to relax from the cares of the year. It has been a time in my life to listen to the voice of God, to allow myself to become quiet and still enough, to hear him speak to my heart. My mornings are quiet because when I get off work it's early with some traffic, but usually a half-hour away, and I'm home having a cup of coffee, and making breakfast (typically toast, eggs, scrambled or over easy, and maybe a few turkey slices). Other mornings it's pancakes and eggs; other times it grits and eggs; and then it could be an omelet. Yes, I like eggs. What makes coffee taste good? To me, it's those creamers. Since the creamers are already sweet, I try not to use sugar, well, maybe a little sugar, but just a little. I like a few cups but I am thinking by next year this time, I will kick the habit altogether, especially if I decide to get my teeth whitened.

What will take the place of coffee? I don't know, I will think of something - maybe green tea? I thought this would be a good time to sacrifice a little bit more than I would ordinarily because I am right at the door of retirement. I may not be in the best shape for retirement, but I am satisfied with all that I have been through with a divorce and still owning the house; I really think I can make it. I want to make sure I have my burial plans intact, not that I am trying to die, but I don't want the kids to scramble, and be off their game, all because I didn't handle my business. So that will be a priority before the year ends.

I just want to talk about how I feel since I am free. I am getting ready for my first cruise, and I am sure I will dedicate some parts of this book to that subject, taking off from Midway Airport to Fort Lauderdale and then off to Miami, 45 min away. I will probably spend the night, a day ahead of time, so I am not rushing. I love the water taxi, so many places to eat and so many beautiful homes to see on the water. I did enjoy the beach, but I was truly afraid of the possibility of getting needled by a jelly fish. That would have been awkward. That was another first-time trip, after my divorce. I didn't stay out late or go places a Christian woman should not go, and I enjoyed the view from the balcony, watching the ships go by in the night, and early morning.

A sister who retired there was in Chicago sometime back in 2015, and I told her I wanted to come to Florida, and although she didn't meet me at the airport, we had dinner, went to Miami, and I visited her church h (Apostolic International Christian Fellowship), I was up every warm morning about 4:30 am, watching the sun come up, so beautiful, I would then take time to walk down to the Starbucks and bring breakfast back to the room, it was so pleasant. Well enough about that particular time in my life.

I notice lately that I have a certain peace; I guess I should explain. I was visiting Nashville, Tennessee somewhere around the beginning of November. Why? Because my kid and his family were moving from Alabama to Nashville. At that time my son, Kenny had an idea that this move would bring them closer to Chicago, and that the movement and hospitality of that state was something he was used to since I had traveled there so many times to work on my music recordings. Even while he was stationed in Alabama, he would ride down to see me and his dad. It was so much fun hooking up, and going to nice restaurants to eat. Not to mention the fine restaurant Monell's, which serves real southern dinner.

But getting back to mornings. I really like waking up no matter where I am, at home, or out of state. It means waking up to another day of mercy, another day of grace, and another day of peace. I shall never forget getting a phone call one day, after realizing that I had to finish this one paper for a final grade in a class I was taking to finish up the semester in 2016. It was a journal type paper, and as soon as I hit the send button, I received a phone call from a relative, telling me some bad news. I was slightly overwhelmed but not totally. I was hurt and despondent and I certainly went into crisis mode; I usually know that because my bladder becomes full quickly until I am destressed.

Before going any further, I want to remember why I mentioned Nashville; I wanted to help with the transition, so I was there for support, to help my son get his babies, my beautiful grandchildren, Kholie and Kenster Jr. in the Nashville systems. I stayed about 5 days, one day longer than I wanted to stay. The boat cruise was six days. But anyway, driving back, I remembered going through Indiana, and I cried out to God about the move Kenny had made for his family, I said to the Lord, "Kenny made this move by faith! Please show up in his life; let his application reach the desk of the person that can make the decision to give him the job in the Veterans Administration office."

At this point, his wife (my daughter-in-law) received her confirmation and had started working in the Nashville school system with benefits as a schoolteacher. (now a principal) Although a few weeks had past, I received a call from Kenster, saying, "Mom I received a letter of commitment." That was part of my prayer! That he was made aware that this move was not in vain, and that God would let him see that he would not allow him to make such a move of faith without the Lord showing him that he would honor his faith. I really appreciate that early morning prayer.

Later that day, I was coming through Gary, and I felt a need to cut the radio down or off, and I could hear softly the Holy Ghost saying, "You know after this year, things won't be the same?" I answered, "Yes, Lord." Although I didn't know what all that entailed, I believed the Lord was saying to me, that your family has had a long run, of little to know deaths and you have had no sorrow to report around the holiday season. And that I should prepare myself, as other families have had to do. I understood this to be true, and so it was. So that day I went home and slept well, and I took time to finish my homework paper that early morning, but leading up to that morning I made preparations to have thanksgiving dinner at my house, just as I had done November 2015.

Robert Jackson Jr., my half brother gave the Thanksgiving prayer. We took pictures and everything, but for some reason, I was in doubt about who would pray this year. I went to church that Sunday and Robert came to second service, and I came to first; I wanted to stay for the two services but I also wanted to see William (my son). So instead, I took him out to noodles not knowing that Robert called. I called him back that Sunday afternoon and he answered saying, "Hey, Sis, I was going to come see you; he mentioned Thanksgiving, asking me how many guests were going to come, I explained and told him about 12 in total, which included my mom, Kenny, came in with Khloe, Jerade my oldest son, Jean (play sister) Gwen, my best friend and maybe are other brother Ivan Sr., and William. I was about to call him back to ask if he wanted Iván to come, too because he'd been worried about him.

While on the phone with him, my head started hurting really bad, which was something rare and not normal, so I cut the conversation saying, "I will see you Thursday". I didn't want it to be in any kind of dispute with him, I just suddenly felt extremely tired. Later that day, I felt like I needed to call him back. When I called Monday night, around 9:15 pm, he didn't answer, and when he didn't answer I tossed through the night. Early the next morning I finished my final paper, hit the save button and heard Georgia saying, "Robert Jackson Jr. had died, and Iván was there with him when it happened."

I was so sad, but it didn't stop there. "Your dad is waiting for you to take him to the hospital, Illinois Masonic" she continued.

The news was more than I could bear and I went into crisis mode immediately. I tried to hold it together, but it was not the norm. It was not going to be the same and the Holy Spirit had taken the time to share this with me; although I didn't want to understand, I did. I appreciate the fact that God in his infinite mercy would take the time to warn me ahead of time that things were about to change and shift. How many times have I been totally shocked, when I had to say goodbye to relatives? Not many, because God had always taken the time to give warning.

I remember a few years back when Robert was in the county hospital, and I went to see him, I prayed for him, and I rebuked the devil trying to take his life. I don't know if our mother was able to notice how serious it was, but I saw death messing with him, and I did rebuke the enemy in the name of Jesus. I often wonder, if he had come by that Sunday and I had put the holy oil on him would that had made it better or did the Holy Ghost speak once and for all concerning the matter, of Robert Jackson Jr's time. Robert couldn't answer me that day, when I called him, November 21, 2016 around 9:15 pm; his voicemail said, "His voicemail was full." His fiancé called him, my dad (Mr. Jackson) had called, no answer, he couldn't answer, he was busy leaving us; he was busy making his last walk with life as we know it. And pronounced dead in the field at 10:05 pm. Dead On Arrival. He was with the one person he wanted to be with – his brother Ivan. They both headed out the door to take mom shopping for food, even thou I had already prepared the Thanksgiving meal.

Good morning Robert. It's not the same without you. I went to church on Thanksgiving Day, and I cried like a baby. Mom didn't go to church, and refused to come to Thanksgiving dinner, but instead had dinner of her own in your honor. Good morning Robert. Are you breathing ok now? Are you looking down on all of us and laughing because we expected you for the holiday, and God expected you home with Him? The bible says (all souls are mine). Kjv. You are a soul, you are His. Do you miss us too? Will we know you when we get there? I am sure your mother cried too. But I tear up every time I think of you, I believe once I teared up less than before; I will be healing soon. But for now, I didn't mind thinking of you the way I do. You were so brave, and I am so sorry I didn't lay hands on you that Sunday.

It's my watch. I am the watch lady on the wall for my family to live and be safe, not because I am the police lady, but because I am the guard for the family; he raises up another in my stead. My cousin, Spencer had the watch for so long and now she is about 82 years old, and certainly not the same. I miss talking to her about the entire family. When I got saved some 38 years ago, I went to her house first, in Oak Park Illinois (member of Christ Temple Church 14 S Ashland Ave.). Mother Gaines (her mother) was living then. Mom and Pap Gains saw more than 75 years of their wedding anniversaries.

Good morning, Robert. Do you see Mother Gaines? She and her husband are there; our great-grandmother Amanda is there (she died at

93 years old). Grandmother, I love you and because you raised me so well, I think the Lord showed you mercy and grace, "love you."

I am Apostolic, and we don't believe in talking to the dead, but in this case, this is a book, and this is an expression, so please indulge me in my dialogue to try to understand some of the mysteries of life, and parting the life. Dealing with pain, working toward the healing place.

The bible tells us that love is stronger than the grave, and it is. You can't take the memories away, you can't take the last conversation away, you can't make it fade, you can't say that it never happened because it did. And you love, love is just that, love. When love is taken away, it hurts, no matter how it happens, loss, breakups, one person outgrows another, it just hurts. Consider love to be a challenge, not a mishap, not just hurt only, but as an eye opener. Embrace love; capture it whenever you can and when it is rejected, look for another way to give love, show love. Love is what it is and I am a sucker for it every single time. And it's ok. Because Christ makes up for it by loving me the way no other can. I will find a way to share it, give it and capture its essence, for the sake of the gospel. (Holy Love) agape love.

I remember that once upon a time, God shared his love with me. I mean, He really showed me something; it was wonderful but frightening. During the time my ex-husband left me, I was so broken, and hurt and tender, but too frightened to be bitter, and so afraid that I would never be whole again. I cried out to God, in a way that I never knew existed, but what I needed was given to me. I didn't need money, although I was blessed to have a good stepmother to step in, I mean my fellowshipping moments with God were truly awesome. When I speak of this love, I mean for a few minutes out of the day, the Lord of Host showed me how much He loves us. I remember thinking, *Since there's so much hatred in the world, if we practiced love this way it would be trampled over more than one human being could express.*

Should we get discouraged because I saw this? No. The bible tells us to guard our hearts, and also to not cast our pearls to swines. He also tells us to shake the dust from our feet and allow our peace to return to us when we are not received (KJV). We continue to be kind, but just know we do not have to worry about being mistreated, we must be vigilant, prudent and careful who we trust, who we give our secrets to and who we share our hearts with. For the time will come when we can love as we should, love without being taken advantage of, and without feeling that we are putting more in than can be administer to usward.

Remember this: God's love for us and the way He wants us to love is very similar to a mother's love. I know some mothers walk away, but most mothers are just that MOTHERS. The church called and asked me to go to Christ Hospital to visit a Mother. This mother had 10 children 6 girls and 4 boys; I observed each one of those children. They showed their mother much love and compassion, and was very glad to see a minister from ACOG (Apostolic Church of God).

Are you tired? Are you weary? Do you miss Mama? I know someone who will love you better than your mother. Are you tired of working or tired of not working? Are you weary of life from so many battles and blows? Are you missing your mama? Let me introduce you to Jesus. He takes good care of the lillies in the field – see how beautiful they are early in the spring! This lets you know that there is hope as they bring life.

I don't truly have the answer, but only a glimpse at what it's all about. It's all about the love of God in our lives. I know He talked to Adam in the cool of the day, but the bible talks about seeking the Lord early in the morning, and as God revealed Himself and time went on, it became apparent that many of the prophets and prophetesses sought God early. The bible says, "Seek him early and call upon him while he is near".

In my first book, I talked about how I would leave this world: *I came here early in the morning a little after 6am in August 1955, and I will leave here quiet and early in the morning. I will slip away, hopefully my family and friends will be close by and I would have lived enough and loved enough and cared enough and seen my kids, kids' kids, and I know then I will be ready to go...ready to see all my family, and love ones of the body of Christ, but most of all Jesus the Christ, who died in my place, and as the song says his love ran red, his love was more than one could experience from a life time of friends, lovers and the sort.*

I don't know when the pain went away, I just know I stopped crying, I stopped fasting, I stop singing so hard, and started laughing, and I got happier than I ever had been since I was on my own before and after marriage.   I felt alive and early in the morning I felt God wrapping me up in his arms. He was right there hiding me, guiding me, protecting me and keeping me. And his love ran red, just for me. Will I ever fall in love again? Probably, and when I do, I hope he loves Jesus like I do. Then, we can get up early in the morning and give God praise. The

God of gods, the Savior of the world. The keeper of my soul, the "Great I Am". Let us pray about this thing call love.

Let us pray about how good God is to us. Let's pray about why we need Him to keep being in our lives.

Dearest Abba, oh how I love You, for Your tender mercies that You offer me, and the whole universe. I shall never cease to mention Your name wherever there is opportunity to tell a dying world how wonderful Your Name is, and how You make daily, weekly, and yearly provision for all of Your creation. To the complete body of Christ, even before many people - men, women, boys and girls are aware of your presence and the love you give to each of them. Let this prayer radiate to the many who do not believe in Christ as Lord, who was hung on a cross, buried in a borrowed tomb, and rose on the third day according to the scripture, just like he said he would. Give victory today, and help everyone in need of your extended care receive you today by faith. In Jesus' name we pray, Amen.

I am so proud of Josh. He's doing good, and I look forward to spending time with him and his family. Just think, next year I will be moving toward my destination of retirement and then I can write anytime I get ready. I usually awaken early in the morning around 05:30 am, now I am up all-night long, and finished this one chapter because I am up and have a little wiggle room to get this chapter done. I am wishing for a cup of coffee right about now, and so I will make a cup of decaffeinated coffee, with some vanilla creamer, and a touch of sugar, not much. Watch the news and doze in my den, before heading off to sleep or to take a bath. And then head off to work.

SCRIPTURE FOR THIS MORNING: *The fear of the lord is the beginning of knowledge, but fools despise wisdom and instruction.* Proverbs 9:10 KJV

CHAPTER 3

Weight vs. Wait

When you think of carrying a weight on your shoulder, what comes to mind? Perhaps, you recognize weight as being something you are dealing with or can't shake off. Is it like a potpourri of situations in your life? Is it like you are carrying someone's load – your personal problems or issues? How exactly do you see the load or weight and cares that life may bring to your door? To your heart? To invade your life?

Weight is described in God's word as the cares of this world. Lay aside things that will deliberately take you down; make you livid; interfere with your rest, sleep and/or peace. Lay aside things that you can't fix or change. Recognizing how difficult it may seem to just let the weight go, or let go of trying to fix the problem even though it is completely out of your control. Let that problem go.

"Therefore, since we are surrounded by so great a cloud of witnesses, let us also lay aside every weight and sin, which clings so closely, and let us run with endurance the race that is set before us. (Hebrews 12:1). The witness that Jesus is the Christ, and He is our savior, redeemer, and kinsmen. We are surrounded by people who have our same dreams and motives behind the things we as Christians do. The cloud of witnesses compensates the cloud of unbelief. Let us set in motion how that Christ died for us and the ungodly, which we were also. Now, our witness and testimony is that He saved us, and raised us up from the place of obscurity and despondency, we now have a part in Him, within, because of Calvary. Let Calvary represent the actual suffering that we face on a daily basis, which is nothing in comparison to what Jesus faced for us at Calvary. Let Calvary represent the weighted wealth and prosperity in the world when others go without food and miss meals frequently, and we can 't understand the miss measurements of humanity.

What am I saying? In short, I am saying that we all have a cross to bear. Jesus was hated, and we shall be also; Jesus was mistreated and so shall we. He died for our sins – past, present and future. We must die daily as Paul so lovingly tells us of our stance and how to own it.

Own what? In this profound passage of scripture, Paul is saying to us; 1) Let Christ be our example. Let him show you through the Holy Ghost, how to deal with weights. First, take them off. Once you have been baptized and filed with His precious gift of the Holy Ghost.

2) We are in a learning process. He despised the shame, so we can despise the way we are treated and singled out for the sake of the gospel. We see this opportunity to be like Christ in unity; we are not standing alone. We are a part of our Lord. Not to get ahead of myself, but I say that He despised the shame as He bore and bares the cross, as He took on the sins of the world by the blood that was shed for us. Because He is the only innocent sacrifice, the only sacrifice that God would recognize and accept. He is the sacrifice that transcends through

generations and is reachable. He has an open-door policy. "Take up your cross and follow me." He is young as this hour; He is as old as the

beginning, before God said "let us make man." Wow. He is my Lord. He was able to look into time to see you and me, and that is why He died for us.

So, as we travel through this life, Christ has traveled through time, never missing anything, because His blood was already applied to our lives, our world, our circumstances, our pain and misfortune. I found out recently that laying aside every weight includes issues that impede our progress toward kingdom building and kingdom work, because His blood has impacted our lives for eternity.

Let us look again at the word *cloud*. In the old testament, the cloud was for the children of Israel. The memory and that love affair with God's children continues even though we have been adopted. You and I were on the byways and He scooped us up for the kingdom, making us royalty; making us above the things that harbor pass mistakes, failures, dilutions and monstrosities.

What is with this blood thing? It is a precious wonder. Because of the sting of death, the strong influence sin had upon the world after infecting our parents Adam and Eve. We were doomed. That is why Paul boldly said in Romans 7:24, *Who shall save me from the sting of death and the old wretched person that I am?* He is now believer in the death, buria,l and resurrection of our Lord and Savior, Jesus Christ.

Is Jesus your Savior? Make him your Savior today. He wants to give you not just life but everlasting, abundant life. You may say, "Suppose I do something wrong?" Well, you will do something wrong. But in this book, I want to stress the importance of knowing who Christ is in the earth. In you and the collaborating of the Holy Ghost working through each believer for the kingdom of our Lord. This is one of the reasons God does not want us to think more highly of ourselves, but as we work our world through Him. He will give us those persons He wants us to influence for the good of the kingdom. We have assignments. Sometimes we are aware of them and other times we come to the light of that mystery. Father has given his word to us to follow, us He makes it clear, that this is a one-way ticket, which is purchased through the blood of Jesus. We now live this life of faith by Gods grace.

You have the blood and you have life. That life is only in the Son of the living God. His mission was accomplished when He became the sacrificial lamb once and for all, the only worthy and solid promise to eternal life, and from up and out of sin's death trap. After Adam and Eve were put out of the garden, God killed an animal. Why? To provide for them. He became a covering for them; He was still looking out for them. You might say after they left the garden, the church began.

The leaves were not enough to cover the man and his wife, so God used the skin of animals to cover their sin and from that point, man has needed a covering. Today, that covering is the only begotten Son of the Father, full of grace and truth. What do you have to do to get this covering for your sins? For this heavy weight of bad mistakes? This heavy weight of lustful things? This bad mistake of wanting and needing sex, out of contents of marriage? This bad mistake of lying, stealing, murdering and doing and selling drugs? This sin of hating me? Hating yourself because of skin color? Because of pride, and lack of respect? THE ANSWER IS TO ACCEPT Jesus as your Lord and Savior. In him we hope and we have life, and we have the blood covering.

Again, as I did in book one, let me invite you to the cross. *At the cross where I first saw the light, and the burden weight of my heart rolled away.* I want you to be honest when you get there. Tell Jesus how bad it is, or tell Him how good it is. He will show you what you will need to do to make your transition in being born again. Jesus said 'Though a man die yet shall he live." (John 11:25). Get rid of that weight. And let the glory cloud that holds the souls of brothers and sisters in Christ who have dropped sins (weights) for the sacrificial offerings of now being able to present our bodies, which have been covered by the blood of the lamb as a living sacrifice holy unto God. It is not a strain or a harsh sacrifice; it is something you have to do. It is done with joy and with a fight for the things that are pleasing to the Lord.

Let us pray: Father, we thank you now for the many blessings you have given to us, and the word map that leads us to peace and safety for such a wicked and difficult time we now live in. We know that as winter turns to spring, You have not forsaken us. You are alive, in our hearts and in our minds, and in all of Your creation. We cannot fix the evil that has been evoked by the forces of evil, but we know because of Your blood, we shall reach our goals and destiny along this journey. We recognize your supernatural power moving in our lives to change lives and to bring men and women, boys and girls who are hurting to your place of refuge and healing and to the new birth that is promised to everyone who believes on the name of Jesus Christ our Lord and king throughout eternity. In Jesus' name we pray.

Let us pray: I realize this is such a little thing to do, and yet so hard, Father, to wait on you. In the process being obedient, help us to grow, and stay in a place where we can flow with You, learning the turn of Your train and following You as we wait, listening for You, as we wait. Longing for you, oh Lord as we wait, In Jesus' name we pray. Amen.

Since we have a clear understanding of what weights are, let us now discuss the other "wait". Psalms 27:14, "Wait on the Lord and be of good courage." It is probably a very difficult thing to do, but we learn discipline when we wait. When we wait on the Lord, we learn a very valuable lesson. We learn that He will come through for us.

I remember asking God for something, and waited for years. Did I get it? No. Perhaps, God had answered me and I didn't want to let the weight go and didn't see that the wait was over. Once I got it, I must tell the truth, I cried and boohooed. I laid out but I want you to know in all of that, I felt the love of God covering me. I felt closer, and more loved for Him not giving me what I asked for after finding out it was not good for me and it was not in God's will. Do I still want it? Ah yeah, but I shall refrain with joy, I shall refrain with peace; I shall refrain now knowing that just because my natural person wants it doesn't mean I supposed to have it or even yield to it.

"Seek ye first the kingdom of God" as instructed in Matthew 6:33. Whatever He wants me to have will be better than what I want for myself. I like God's plan, and I have learned that usually when He is silent, I am not going to receive my request. However, I can assure you that when He speaks on the matter, you will be well aware of His hand on your life. You will learn to wait until He moves in you, for you and brings to you what He has for you from His perfect will. I wanted His permissive will, but there will come a time that you must prepare yourself to step out directly on the perfect will of God. That is a place you will find through fasting, praying, reading and meditating on His word. God's spirit will move on your behalf because you will not fight against His holy presence. How long will the process take? Well, I must say that is something that the Lord through your worship regime will reveal and when this happens, you will know.

Finally, I want to leave you with some encouraging scriptures on this topic of waiting:

- "Wait for the lord and keep his way" (Psalms 37:34)

- "I waited patiently for the Lord: he inclined to me and heard my cry" (Psalms 40:1)

- "I am weary with my crying out: my throat is parched. My eyes grow dim with waiting for my God." (Psalms 69:3)

- "I wait for the Lord, my soul wait, and his word, I hope." (Psalms 130:5)

CHAPTER 4

What a Set Up

It was a bright, shiny day; it was right after the passion of Christ, and the women found the tomb empty. I can feel it in the air, every time I read this passage of scripture, because He rose in me. The angel of the Lord met them, advising them to the fact that Jesus is no longer dead. The account of the event can be found in St. Luke, chapter 24. So, they went away, radiant and full of life to tell his disciples "he is a risen."

Jesus was very excited about His new body. Although his body was both human and divine before, it didn't compare to what it was after the Resurrection. I believe he could appear and disappear, but now that He was going home, He had a few things left to tidy, here on earth. He needed to ensure His pupils knew that He'd risen, and that their job was to make sure the gospel message was spread throughout the world. They needed to know where to go in order to receive this power, to spread His message throughout the world. This mission was strategic, "It is finished." What is finished? The sacrificial Lamb, the only sacrifice God would except for all humanity once and for all. Jesus ransomed us from sin, and death, now the soul of man has a home, because Jesus shed blood of us. Our souls raptured from hell, no longer afraid of death.

Truly the Calvary cross work was done, and He was again going home to sit at the right hand of His father. Wow! How exciting. You may ask, "How do you know it was exciting?" Well, let's look at the facts, and you can draw you own conclusion. Keep in mind, I am trying to get you to see it from another perspective, and although the scripture is of no private interpretation, I am glad to write about this, and would even love to preach this message again someday. (smile)

He joins the men who are disciples, and they know something is up, but they don't know what it is. They really want Jesus to stay with them as they tell him, who they think is a stranger in the city, about the crucifixion of their Lord. The men just took for granted that Jesus was a visitor, and stranger in the city as they were walking the road of Emmaus, because He didn't seem to know what was going on, or so they thought. Jesus began to speak to them about Himself, how and why He would come to die and rise again, beginning with Moses and the prophets. But they didn't know it was Jesus.

Jesus was willing to opt out of the group, but they were compelled and wished for Him to fellowship with them even longer. As the Lord breaks bread with them they were aware it was Messiah! But before their eyes were opened, they received a private bible class from Jesus himself. The men acknowledged their hearts were on fire, with enthusiasm after He imparted the words of life, while traveling on the road, saying, "Did not our hearts burn within us," as he expounded in the scripture.

Once he breaks bread, they recognized him; He didn't give them time to further investigate. He had vanished, left in his new body, just as he joined them, now He was gone. Perhaps He didn't want to try to convince them any further. Maybe He missed talking and seeing his disciples. By now the women let them know, that He was not dead but alive eternally. Maybe it was just good to be alive indefinitely. Whatever it was, He was gone, for moment.

What a comeback, what a setup. Here, Jesus spends three days in the heart of the earth, and has completed His mission, past every satanic test, having church with those that died before, He came to earth, born of the virgin, Mary. Teaching and feeding the multitude hated of the priesthood, assinated by the Roman government, and now holds all power in heaven and earth in His hands. Now, He has the keys to death, hell, and the grave. Now, the blood of Jesus is applied to all that believe on His name. Was He not still humble and compassionate? Yes, He was, but this time He had a mandate; this time part two the mission is set in motion: "The Great Commission."

Before entering heaven, a place he knows as home, He wanted to make sure the gospel message was in place, as planned. He wanted to make sure that His people, the 120, would be in the upper room at the right time on the right day, so they would all be filled with the gift, that He promised, the gift that would pass from generation to generation. The precious gift of the Holy Ghost, so that they would be able to proclaim that Jesus was born, died, and rose, and has all power, and through this historical event we born to righteousness, son and daughter of the highest through the forgiveness of sins, by his own precious blood, a sacrifice that only God would except, for sin's debt. His death, burial, and resurrection were the stories that would be proclaimed to generation to generation. Satan's attack on men and women would be destroyed forever.   On that great day, God himself will pick the date and time; that day and hour of Armageddon no one knows. But it will come. We all will stand before the judgement seat of Christ to give an account of the deeds done in this body, and others will stand before the Great White Throne. The reward is for those who have not made Jesus their choice, waiting too late or allowing him to slip away from their heart. For the day you hear his voice the bible says in the book of Psalms, "harden not your hearts."

When Christ speaks, listen and as He leads you to your assignment, walk toward the light, let your heart turn to Him for your cleansing from sin and shame. For now, you may go before the throne of grace, take Him your cares, your faults and insecurities. Look to Jesus now, by faith, He is waiting to give you your assignment. He has been coaching you along the way. Don't turn away. Take his hand now; it can only be done by faith. Until he returns, the fight for righteousness is in full gear. For the battle is already won. The bible speaks to us, encouraging us to fight the good fight of faith. Until then the fight for right and righteousness will be fought by the power of the Holy Ghost.

Most Christians and theologians believe Jesus stayed on the earth for 50 days, with many witnesses. That too is my belief. Let's check out this body, the one you and I will receive one day. Jesus reappears in his glorified body. Before the Lord would be caught up in the clouds, Jesus had to make sure the disciples knew that the Comforter would be with them as He was, before He received His new body. The Holy Ghost would guide them into all truth, the investment was great. His own life His precious blood, paid for the transformation and irrevocable protection from death, hell, and the grave.

Many have heard or seen the movie, "Passion of the Christ". That blood, that precious blood of Jesus was for our ransom. Jesus paid my sins' debt and I am glad that now I am free to live righteously, not because I am righteous, but that He made me to be righteous. I believe He took my sins away, when He died for me. Although this was tragic, and the suffering was overwhelming, I believe this because the bible says they beat him and spit on him, and beat him till blood came streaming down, for you, and for me. They gambled for His garment, and put a crown of thorns on His head, just for you and for me.

Jesus now appears to the Disciples; He didn't knock on the door, or announce His entry. He did it just the way He does it now - He just shows up, and fills every space. He is everywhere at the same time without getting our lives confused with anyone else's. How do I know that? Because when we are born or when we die there is a record. The bible tells us there is a book. We are in that book; if we have been born again, it's called, "The Book of Life."

Not one time but several times, does Jesus appear, and each time He becomes more glorified. The angels are nearby, and the longer He is on the earth, the more glorified He becomes. At this point, the first sermon had been preached, since He is alive again forever. The women went back telling all the men, our Lord is risen and is no longer dead.

How do you feel when the door bell rings unexpectedly? Does it throw you off balance? Are you curious? Do you ignore the door bell? Do you run and open the door? Or, cautiously check to see who it could be?

I remember once, when I was kid, Mom and Dad were at work (this was before I went to live with my grandmother,) Robert Jr., Ivan and myself were in the rear of the house. As soon as the door bell rang, somewhere around 5:00pm or a little later, I ran to the door, and cautiously looked through the curtain. The door was sturdy with that old glass top where you could really see who was on the other side. The man was tall, extremely fat and had a newspaper in his hand.

Although the door was locked, I began to shake to my knees and screamed; the boys came to the door and screamed, too. I then gathered us together and went to the side window in the rear (in the dinning room) and yelled out the window to Mrs. Moss, and asked if we could stay with her and her family until our mother came home because were so frightened. I was so afraid I never wanted to go back home again. We all climbed out the window trembling. Our mother was angry that we went to the neighbor's house. I could only imagine what would have happened had we opened the door. The man was 35-45 yrs. old; he was wearing an ivory (or dingy white) hat, a light-colored short sleeve shirt, and some dark colored pants. What a horrific situation. It took a little time to get over that doorbell shock.

If my bell rings now I can tell whether or not it's a good ring, or a threat of some kind. When I get to heaven, I am not going to ask Jesus who that was; I am just glad I didn't open the door.

But speaking of the door, Jesus doesn't ring the door bell; He doesn't even knock on the door. This is a man both human and heavenly, and He comes through the door exercising His power and authority. This same Jesus who said He has the keys to death, hell, and the grave. So, why knock? While the disciples were all gathered together discussing the events of the day, Jesus appeared to Simon, and stood among the disciples and said to them "Peace be with you." They were all frightened and thinking that they saw a ghost. The Lord needed them to believe, and not be afraid or doubt the power of His resurrection.

At this point, Jesus takes center stage and told His disciples to handle Him, showing them the nail circles in His hands and feet, the piercing in His side. Although they were not used to this new glorified body, Jesus assured them that a ghost does not have flesh and bones; they were overjoyed with amazement. We now know that although He had a glorified body, He still had an appetite for some food, as Jesus ate some broiled fish in their presence. The bible does give us the incident with the two disciples on the road of Emmaus, where He breaks bread with them. Jesus begins to speak to them as if He was in another dimension of life. He said, "This is what I told you while I was still with you."

He elaborates on the law of Moses and the prophets. "The Messiah will suffer and rise from the dead on the third day; and repentance for the forgiveness of sin shall be preached in His name to all nations beginning at Jerusalem. Jesus goes on to teach them about the power of witness, to elaborate on the time that Jesus was here on the earth. The Lord needed to get their minds on heavenly things. No more hiding, scared to speak out. It was time to spread the true and living gospel. The time was now!

In the book of Acts, Jesus explains to them that they should tarry in Jerusalem until they are filled with power from on high. Once Jesus gave them the Great Commission, the Lord was taken up and He was hidden in the clouds; the disciples continued to look for him. Two angels stood beside them asking, "Why stand here looking for Him?

This same Jesus who has been taken from you into heaven, will come back in like manner." KJV, NIV.

Once the group of 120 were in the upper room they received power that came to them like a mighty rushing wind, with cloves of fire that set upon each of them, and they began to speak in other tongues as the spirit of God gave them utterance. (NIV). I can never get enough of how the Lord gave us this great gift of faith, to receive His power to witness to light up a room with His presence when we are led and ushered by the Holy Ghost. The late Andre Crouch wrote a song. *Tell them... even when we witness, we are exercising a great love for our brothers and sisters who may not know the Lord, and need a hand of encouragement.* So, let us tell them inspire them, persuade them, to know who Jesus is. Let us convince them that Jesus is Lord. Needless to say, this gospel message has gone around the world, and everyone knows Jesus is alive and well. And everyone prays to him secretly at one time or another. For fear they have missed the light. (John 1) KJV.

I am not sure if this book will yield to us the two most important men in the bible that opened up the way for Jews and Gentiles alike to receive this great new life. I believe one of the goals of the Holy Ghost is to encourage us in the middle of antagonism, cult and pagan worship.

Let us take time to pray right now:

Father, we thank you for the gospel, for this gospel makes sense; it has helped us to follow the path You have set in place for Your people to follow. Lord, You not only want us to have this great joy and peace we find in receiving the Holy Ghost, but You want us to share the love. We

49

thank you Lord, for the many souls and lives we all can touch in our lifetime. Blessings and honor belong to You. I hear the song, "Oh, how I love Jesus because He first loved me." Thank you for looking down on us, working in us and through us to fulfill Your purpose, which is to bring Your creation into this marvelous light. Jesus lives... He lives within my heart. Yes, we serve a risen Savior who insists that we join Him around the table. Father, You have prepared a home in glory for us; we will sit at Your feet and be blessed. After so many kingdom moments, (1000 yr reign) we will settle back here on a new heaven and new earth. We appreciate the wonders of Your love. In Jesus' name we pray. Amen.

In book one I spoke of the out pouring of God's love for me. I was so thankful as I softly moved by faith, I had no idea where this faith was taking me. I was 23 years old at the time and felt dirty, awkward and on a path toward hell. I was so convinced that I was a nobody and that there was no way I could reach any level of faith, even the faith I had as a child. I was feeling the heat of not having God's love, I had not heard His voice in three years, so I thought I was doomed. Although I was not saved, I could not ignore the trees, the winds, the moon, or the wonderful sunlight on my face. I could not ignore how He has protected me. I could not ignore my conscious telling me there is a God, and that I will one day have to answer to Him. I need to seek Him, look for Him to show me the way.

I was broken, battered, torn and needed the love that only He could give me. I had one other encounter with God; although He didn't speak, I knew He was there. I was angry that I could not find Him, but then He reached down with His infinite mercy, to let me know He was in the room with me while I was in a very confused state in my life. While walking one day, I heard him softly say, "Deborah, I am going to save you." Now 38 years later, I am glad I listened to that wonderful still small voice. The one that speaks to your soul. It cannot be denied. The voice that says, "I see your flaws, your ups and downs, where you are falling short. I see that you want to know why things are not working and going your way. Was it a set up? I am here to help you, and give you life, because you are not alive. You need me because you have come to the end of yourself. You have no hope, and I am come to bring you to a place of peace, and rest." You are all bald up inside and cannot unclench your fist. You are always ready to fight a losing battle.

I am so glad I found this hope in Jesus. This hope will not let us be ashamed. I sojourned to stay washed to feel Him over and over again. When you first find Jesus and He speaks to you, you feel such a love for humanity. You want to tell everyone, every time you leave the house. Jesus is alive. Do you know Jesus? He's alive! I am forgiven, let me take you to him; let me introduce you to this man. It is not enough for me to have this hope, and other witnesses too, but it is important that each believer have this hope and we must go into all the world and tell everyone we know and meet, that Jesus has a plan mapped out entirely for them. You can depend on Father to be there in your best moments, as well as the most arduous times in your life.

Will Jesus wait until you are at the bottom before he steps in...is that the set up? Not really, He will take control and work in you His will. He calls for you and me and He knows us by name. Let us not ignore His pleading even after we have come to know him more. Let us learn to trust him, let us learn to obey him, and it will be well with our souls.

CHAPTER 5

What Time Is It

Time to be born, for some babies the moment was perfect. Mothers and fathers planned the precious event; holding the precious bundle was all worth the problems and pain of delivery. Just recently, a young woman came forward, after she realized she had been kidnapped from the hospital where she was born. Her parents missed her and pretended she was readily available to them. By this, I mean they had birthday parties in her name, believing that she was still alive, and that one day they would see their daughter again. The woman who stole the child dressed as a nurse, went into the nursery and took the child out of the hospital and raised her as her own flesh and blood.

It was discovered some 18 years later this young woman found out that she was taken against her parents' wishes and that she was always in their hearts. She told the media, "I will visit my mother in jail, and I will get to know my parents from this point on." She was not angry that she had been stolen; she seemed to love her life, and her upbringing. Her reaction to her mom, who was facing a stiff penalty for the charge, was that of compassion. Most times, it may be difficult to bite the hand that feeds you. I cannot say that she won't need therapy or that she is mature enough to sort this out or that she will get Christian counseling, but what I do know is that she was brave enough to stand in front of the cameras to let the media know she was not going to let this incident, as tragic as it was, define her.

Time to learn a lesson (although this was an unbalanced wave of events): the mother who really wanted her, took this child and apparently raised her as her own. Crazy I know, but it happened just like that. Her true mother and father never stopped hoping for the return of their daughter. Time proved that this young lady would do what was right in her eyes, which was not to abandon her mother and yet venture out to know and learn the parents she never knew. If there is a lesson to be learned here, it must be that this child has a level head, and is a willing participant in doing what she feels is right regarding this nightmare that is only now ending for her real parents. She had no control over why and when this happened.

I don't know if I looked for her to be angry or even reluctant, I just see a well-balanced person, who doesn't seem to have been abused in any way. Of course, there is no excuse to steal someone's child or take anything that isn't yours, and I am not condoning the mother's behavior. I am recognizing, however, that no matter how wrong this was, this young lady is not going to stop living and will probably unwrap her new gift of having another set of parents. I could say one good and one bad, but only God knows and the law knows and now she has to pay for her mistake some 18 years later. She is doing time and may take comfort in knowing she raised this baby to become a beautiful young woman, or she will have time to think about how selfish she was to take someone's baby as her own. (Harlem Hospital 1987, written by Lindsey Ellefson 5:34pm January 18, 2017. The article show that the young woman defended her mother's actions, and yet acknowledged it was wrong.)

Time for the 21-day Daniel Fast. I did the fast last year. I am pleased to say, that although I didn't care for the Daniel's fast, it gave me enormous strength to really let some baggage go that was weighing me down. I knew I would have supernatural strength, and it came just about the time that I had an unction I would need it. Although we were given a choice to do two other type of fasting, I believe that since I was single, this one would prove more reasonable since I didn't have anyone or anything to stand in my way.

The Daniel Fast is a more consecrated fast and more sacrificial for me. The elimination fast would be ideal for those celebrating Valentine's Day, or on a specific diet or married. The third type is the media fast; although tempting, this fast wouldn't work for me because it's not practical. I work using computers; there are at least three computers at my desk at work, and if I bring a personal computer, that would make four not to mention my phone. Looking up zip codes for reports, vehicle information and other important types of media facts I need at my fingertips, doing a tour of duty.

It's time to tell yourself, "I am beautiful", "I am handsome", "I am worth it", and "I am going to do what God would have me to do, not for myself, but so that it will be well with me; I desire to please the Lord". It's time to look to Jesus, and depend on Him to walk the walk with us, and talk the talk with us, so that we can be free from all of the dangerous darting games of the enemy (Satan). I know he doesn't usually attack us directly but sometimes he will. He will send a fleet when breaking up your home and setting traps, but when you and I pass too many tests I believe he comes not because he wants us, but because he is familiar with our kind. And his kingdom depends on our bondage, to sin death hell and the grave. Let us continue to look to Jesus, who is the author and finisher of our faith. If we pass too many tests, the devil is aware that we can do damage to his kingdom by raising a holy and genuine DNA generation for the body of Christ. I believe that our personal obedience to Christ is a true and excellent way to advance the bloodlines that we come from. When we teach our children and grandchildren to recognize their creator and get to know Him, this behavior threatens the kingdom of darkness. That is why Satan uses principalities by putting more liquor stores in our communities and propositioning drug users. He wants to train men and women to be dealers because it follows a generational curse. They are under the influence and bondage of sin with blood on their hands by selling, killing, and stealing from those who have become prey for their habits and advancement in the satanic kingdom in which they themselves may not even have a clue, in being apart of this worlds culture.

A time to make up your mind. If you follow Satan, he will do all he can through his intentional and his heavenly earthly realm (power of the air) to prevent you from being free. He makes your body sick - ask Job. He can affect your finances and suck all the life out of you, hoping you will stop trusting and depending on God. Ask the woman with the issue of blood. Please don't think because I have brought out some of the tricks of the enemy that I am glorifying his position; I only want you to know that God is still looking on. Remember when Satan asked permission to attack Job? God said, okay, but do not kill him. This was a challenge the devil could not resist. He desired to show God that Job only served Him for what was given him; all those material things. Once the hedge of protection was removed, Satan began working, dragging Job's life, and his accomplishments to death's door.

Fortunately, God knew Job, and Satan could not penetrate Job's hope in God. Job thought he would die, and although his wife said because of his dilapidating health he should just curse God and die, Job addressed her as being foolish. Not only did the devil use his wife but his three closes friends declared him to be a sinner although he hadn't sinned. Job's life changed suddenly and immediately.

When you experience a sudden and immediate negative change, the devil probably had permission to try you. Job passed his test. What kind of test? The test of faith. He passed, and God blessed him suddenly and immediately after the test was over. He had gained double for all that he had lost. His cattle, land, children,(new children) and health were all restored. Although Job's heart was broken and he had not known that God and Satan were deliberating over him, he maintained his faith in God. I believe one of the reasons that Job was so victorious in the face of trial and testing is because he had a relationship with God. He knew Father and Father knew him.

You may ask, Why did it take so long for God to answer Job? Because God was taking him to the highest level of testing. God knew he was presenting a man for the generations of faithful believers. How many times have you pressed on and pushed back the tears because of the story of Job? A servant of God, a man who said, "All my appointed time I will wait on the Lord". A man who realized whether he lived or died, his redeemer lives. When you know that Jesus is alive, you can take it when the doctor has a heart-to-heart talk with you about your disease. You can deal with problems concerning your sickness, your child or your world around you. As you move forward, some takeaways from this chapter is that as long as you wait on your redeemer, He will show up and show out on your behalf; He will not allow the enemy to have his way with you. He will step in after you have been exhausted, after you have suffered and cried out to God for his help. Watch for Him. He is coming your way – softly, tenderly, and with gifts to heal you and refresh your soul. He will hold you and comfort you until it's time to fight again. Until its time to stand up again, for all that is good and perfect in Christ the Lord, for the best you, on earth, while you live.

There is a time for loss, usually before the lesson. There is a time for tears, usually during the lesson. Time for heartache and suffering, usually in the heat of the battle. Knowing that God has not forgotten you, hold your head up because He is getting ready to put you on display and tell the devil, "This one belongs to me."

Remember Jesus has prayed for us therefore we can't help but win. I can hear the song, by Walter Hawkins, *God will open doors for you, fight on through your darkest night.* Sometimes you are encouraged through song or the pastor's message. Sometimes you have to fight through the gray clouds because there may not be anyone to understand. No mother or father, sister or brother, no children – just you and maybe a few "friends" who declare it's your fault and that this fall is because you did something wrong. But the bible declares in the book of Job he did everything right except for being afraid. He wanted his children to be saved. Although they lost their lives, it was truly about Job. The devil already had them, he wanted Job's soul... but Job,was one soul he would never have.

Although it is always time to give God glory, praise and worship, there are times that the thought of worship is so overwhelming wherever it hits you that is where you will praise him. In the grocery store, on the bus, the train, in your car, in your bed. No one may ever know, but you. Why? Because it's your story – how God brought you out of a tormented place; how He lifted your burdens when people you loved and cared for walked away, leaving you to fend for yourself, hoping you would fall or lose it all. But God stepped in and said, "Not so. This one is mine. Mine to serve in the beauty of holiness. Mine to testify in the temple and the high or low places. Mine to witnesses and tell others who I am and what I have done." Our witness and testimony of Father's love is like music to His ears, knowing we are not conformed to this world and refusing to be ashamed of the gospel of Christ. Our witness will recharge our spirits as we prepare for the next fight, the next battle, the next thing to be conquered by the precious blood of the lamb, in Christ Jesus.

Time to fight the giant with Jesus. Jesus is smooth; we need not buckle under when He has already paid for our salvation. We come like David, we come in the name of the Lord. Oh, I know it seems like I have arrived, but I have not. Everyday the devil finds some dark corner of my past and brings it up to me. I must remind myself, *Jesus took my sins away and put my stuff in the sea of forgetfulness.* As I confess my faults, He is faithful and just to forgive me as I refuse to practice sin. Whenever I feel trapped by something I cannot seem to overcome, I take that weakness to Jesus. Tell yourself that you are a winner, victorious and an overcomer. "Greater is He that is in you, than he that is in the world" (1 John 4:4, KJV). I can be strengthening in the inner man because Christ prayed for me that after I am strengthened, I can then strengthen my brother/sister.

Time to bow down and worship. Worship while you are awake, worship while you sleep, worship on your job, in your car and at church. Worship because the Lord is good and His mercy endureth forever. This is a continuation of actions that is meant to be so as we learn and grow, we'll be encouraged to finish the work and the race.

The bible tells us in a parable that the violent taketh by force, how we have to bind the strong man in order to get what we want. Jesus uses the story of how a robber can only come in by force taking and stealing from the owner, the keeper of the house, because no one is going to give you their stuff. So, in order to win over Satan's rule and reign, we must violently take what we want. This kind cometh out but by fasting and prayer; if we want something from God and enter into the devil's camp to regain our possessions, it must be done by force. I am taking back my everything.

What other example do I have to give? Look at the passion people have when they set out to hurt you, you will never get an apology. Why? Because they meant to be violent; rarely is a murderer sorry for killing someone. It was meant to happen as they plotted and planned. Of course, there are some crimes of passion when they see something that takes them over the edge like a lover with another. But it is still violent and is still by force; so likewise is it in the kingdom, I will push out for service as much as I can whenever I can for as long as I can.

Let us pray: Dearest Father, Glory and honor are thine. We love You for the many lessons You have taught us about time. Only You know when You will come back for us; in the meantime, let us work the work You have for us to do. Be with us when storms arise, just like some of the life struggles that Job experienced. Like those Jesus endured as He walked this earth sending the Holy Ghost to help us survive while left here to contend for the faith. I thank you for the Apostles and the doctrine left by the apostolic fathers. We love and adore You. Keep us Lord, and let us tell others of Your marvelous love... let us violently press on till we see You in peace. In Jesus' name we pray. Amen.

CHAPTER 6

Fill In The Blanks

We all have busy lives working to retire. Some are conscious of the idea, but for some it will come as a shock. I was listening to WBBM on the way in to work last night and I heard the journalist say, "If you are a 65-year-old man, you would want to save at least $72,000.00 for your initial retirement and if you are a 65-year-old woman, you would want to save around $96,000.00." I guess the number difference is because women initially live longer than men. These amounts are just extra funds as savings accounts, and a savings account only to meet those needs that may come up as a senior. This could include some minor surgery, or out of pocket costs for related issues, or to help when downsizing and to minimize the cost of everyday living expenses. Perhaps some stock and bonds.

Some of us will stay busy working several jobs to make money so that we can pay for health insurance under the ACA (Affordable Care Act), which will affect the quality of our lives tremendously. Some will work to keep the money flowing in order to prevent the exhaustion of funds and to invest in the market or other business ventures. Some of us will dedicate our beginning senior years to helping our children and our grandchildren. Having extra funds is important during these retirement years because it is more likely than not that our bodies will not be able to withstand all the wear and tear it once did when we were younger.

Finding ways to stay healthy and reduce stress will prove rewarding during our senior years,

Others will dedicate some time doing something they never had time to do while working a career because many career jobs take a lot of energy, and the commitment can be taxing. I don't know for sure, but I believe during these last meaningful working years some think about what they want to do, as well as things they never had a chance to do. Many take into account and realize that since they still have a good portion of their health left, they want to help others, by visiting and feeding the elderly. Needless to say, some seniors will remarry or marry for the first time. I am in agreement with making sure you are happy and making these years count; mind your own business and find ways to be remembered within your family. (smile)

Nothing is wrong with visiting or feeding someone in a nursing home. Some may not know who you are; in their mind, they may think you are their son or daughter that never comes to see or celebrate them. However, that shouldn't stop you from helping. If you sing, you can arrange for a concert. If you read, you can arrange with staff to read a book. Some have dogs to come in and give attention to the elderly. Giving back can be a wellness pill and may work both ways in feeling significant. Our church has started a coat drive, this is our second year(2019).

Is age just a number? You fill in the blanks...but for me, age is a number. Sometimes, I feel it and sometimes I don't. I have to look in the mirror and realize that the lady in the mirror is someone I have known for a long time. She is changing, and yet she is the same. She is a warrior; she has raised her children and doesn't expect them to take care of her when she is old. I know they will offer, but I will do my best to make them proud. I don't want to be a burden. But I thank God for India, my daughter-in law, she will probably make sure I'm ok. (God willing).

One thing I am learning now, is that letting go comes in stages. I have also noticed that God has a way of showing us who we are, where we have been, and where we are going. Sometimes, it's real clear; other times, we overlook it. But when you get quiet and observe your surroundings, you will see the hand of God. You must decide to let go. You must let go once you realize it, and then allow your mind to see yourself through the process.

You will learn how to pray, what to pray for and who to pray for even if you don't know the people you are praying for. Your experiences will cause you to become compassionate. Your own pain and struggles will allow you to spot them at the grocery store, at work, when you enter a room during prayer service, while walking in the mall or having dinner with you significant other even while you are on vacation. When I was a young mother, I just knew the older, mature women could tell whether I was doing a good job of raising my family. If she smiled, I was getting a good grade; if she frowned, I knew I had much more work to do.

You will know how to pray when you see your own past play out in others. Metaphorically, it's like "the stage of life"; we all have a part. Some parts are painful, others are joyous. Sometimes we cry until we give up, give in, give out or find freedom to go on. You can only find true freedom when you find Christ who sets us free from a dark world of "I did it my way." Nothing is wrong in doing it your way; it's just that there is a better way. God's way is not only sweeter, but His way is a sure way of peace and safety no matter what part we have to play on the stages of life. We win in the end because of God's care and love for us through his son, Jesus. No one can hardly resist a good movie and as human beings we are interested in stories. Father knows all the stories of life and He has made us all individually to make decisions about how we play our parts. Since He knows everything, we should consider His way, His plan, on His stage with the breath He has given us. Let us call Him and expect His guidance and protection. Through the blood of our Lord and Savior Jesus Christ.

For the bible teaches us there is no temptation but such that is common to man. My problems have been or will be your problems at one time or another. Have you ever had your lighst out because you could not pay the light bill? I know how that feels. Have your ever went to take a bath and the water was cold? Been there too. If you are graduating from college and it was difficult but you were able to finish, you can pray for someone else to stay encouraged and to stay focused. I realize that some stories are very tragic and harsh and overwhelming - even with support systems in place. But now I want to pray for those who have had very difficult lives even though they are Christians.

Let us pray: Dearest Father, my sisters and my brothers, who are having difficulty hearing your voice and making right decisions in order to get to the next place in their lives need your help now. Please guide them through the Holy Spirit to lead them to a place of stability in you by having a place to pray, cry out, seek You, and receive the anointing of the power of the Holy Ghost. I know your word clearly states that after we suffer awhile, You will establish us and make our way clear. But please reach for the man, the woman, the boy, the girl who don't feel You. Lord, open up their understanding and help them to receive everything you have for them according to your will. For Lord, I know that there is nothing too hard for You. Let them see that You will never leave them and that you are faithful even when none of us are. Please Lord, consider us for we are dust and yet we are royalty. What a great mystery! Help us to open in the spirit realm that we may learn your will for our lives. In Jesus' name we pray. Amen.

This next chapter is dedicated to the memory of Robert Jackson Jr. (1957-2016).

CHAPTER 7

You Can Breathe Now

———————o———————

I remember him asking me for water, I was in the bathroom, 44th and Drexel; it was a third-floor apartment. "Bebba", he couldn't say Deborah, the whole family called me Deborah. I spelled my name that way all through school; there was no "h" on the end of my name. I didn't find that out until I bought my first birth certificate at age 18. Robert was medium brown complexion, nice grade of hair, and wanted me to love him and treat him like we were brother and sister.

I didn't know how to connect with him. I don't remember ever hugging him or loving him as a child. (sister love). But I remember him saying, "Bebba, give me some water please." I was in the bathroom because I had chronic soar throat, walking around with no shoes on in the heart of winter. I was gargling with warm water. So, I would give him warm water and he would say, not warm water, cold water, Bebba! I am sorry I couldn't get that right. The family didn't stay there too long before we moved to 5600 S. Prairie. My family consisted of my mother, Mr. Jackson, and my brothers Robert and Ivan. He seemed to show some type of love I couldn't comprehend. I always felt like I was his mother although we were only two years apart. I was just his big sister.

I guess this notion of feeling motherhood so early is because I was left to care for them more than a little child should. He always obeyed me

66

when I would give him chores to do after school. Sometimes, I would pretend to be sick when we lived on 79th and Green so he would clean the kitchen for me. I was 9 and he was 7. He would wash the dishes for me; both parents were at work. I would come in from school and desire to lay down and watch television. I'd tell him how sick I was and he would wash dishes. After he finished, I'd say, "I'm better now", laughing in his face. Sometimes I really didn't feel good and he would take care of the dishes and I would later play teacher and let the boys do their homework in my room until they would start throwing paper at me.

As the teacher, the youngest didn't care for me much and would start the riff-raff. We all laughed and played, cleaned the house, and messed it up again. We were only kids. Sometimes our parents felt sorry for me putting all that burden on my shoulders and they hired a baby sitter, a little older than me, which proved worse.

Breaking down the love and affection in the family it went like this: My grandmother would call me and she wanted to know what was going on and I told her. She would come over when I was sick to feed me. I had really bad fevers during those young years. Mom gave much of her attention to Robert Jr. because she thought he was overlooked and felt that since he was the darkest in the family that he needed that extra attention. Let's face it, we all love our boys. I didn't see anything wrong with him, but mom would speak about dark men in a negative way. I couldn't understand that because her dad was really dark. Ralph Peek Sr. He owned a little barbecue place in Jew town. But Robert loved his mother and she gave him more support than anyone. I was a bad sister and an undeserving daughter.

Mr. Jackson was the church treasurer and no matter where he would put the little brown bag with nickels quarters and dime and pennies, I'd find it. I would buy candies or cake or white castle burgers. I didn't know how to cook so when I didn't see bologna, I found that bag and bought food to eat because 6:30 in the evening was pretty late for dinner. Sometimes, I would try to blame Robert Jr., but that didn't work. My mom knew it was me. Sometimes, Dad would lash me; it would hurt, but mom was brutal. She would take me in the basement and take all my clothes off and whip me so bad. It was so humiliating and I, to this day must try hard to forget how wicked that felt for just a few little pennies, nickels dimes and quarters. Eventually that stopped and we would start getting an allowance.

I certainly was doing enough work around the house. I deserved an allowance and in my little hateful heart I knew that caring for my brothers so young was too much for me. I had to repeat the third grade. Mom took time off from working to be a stay-at-home mom. When it came to doing homework, it was a disaster. She was screaming at me and I may have known the answer, but she made me feel like a dummy, and she wasn't that smart. Dad eventually took the time to teach me where I struggled the most, which was my time tables. I thank him today for that.

One day I had a dream I had lots of dolls, Barbee and Ken dolls, but they had no clothes; the Woolworth store had doll clothes. Although some of the poor church girls who had no mother suggested that we go steal the clothes, I had the dream that I took the doll clothes and got caught. I knew that dream could come true, but I did it anyway. When we left the Franks department store we also went to the Woolworths.

So, I knew that was not a good idea, I went anyway. I got caught and taken to the 6th district police station and put in lock up, which I believe that was supposed to scare me. Well, needless to say, when mom came to pick me up, I knew I was going to get a beating. The other girl, Gloria, was met by her father's wrath. He beat her right in our house. I never ever saw a person get beat or seen the scars on her body like that in my life. I said to myself I hope he never beats me. As a matter of fact, I remember thinking, *I don't think I will ever steal anything again.* My mother came into my room calmly; I asked her was she going to beat me too, and she said no. The next day I got baptized into the Church of Christ. I never stole again.

Although I am Apostolic and sanctified today, raising children to be right with God's power can be a challenge. After having that dream, it was clear to me that I was not alone. There was someone else besides my parents running things. Robert Jr. had things going on, but he was pretty smart in school. Although I struggled, I could help him and I did by playing his teacher after school. Eventually I was eleven and it was time for change. There was talk that my parents were going to separate. All the family came over little by little to talk mom out of it, but she was head strong and had made up in her mind that she was going to divorce Mr. Jackson and marry the Minister. Dad laughed it off saying, "You are like a daughter to him". So now I hated her again because she was going to do something stupid.

Robert Jr. who was 8-years-old going on 9, boldly said, "I am going with Mom because she needs someone to take care for her/protect her".

Ivan said, at 5-years-old, "I am staying with my dad". Well, bad as I was, I didn't think the pastor was going leave his wife, and I didn't think he was right always being at the house when dad was at work. No matter how all the family tried to make her stay, she had a hard head and refused to see how serious the move would be to her life and the lives of us all. I should have punished myself and went with her, but let's face it, I wouldn't have turned out right. I would not have the good life that I had, which was full of church, my grandmother, my friend-cousins, Saundra and Jerry, and their mom Ruby. I was ashamed of my mother for not loving her family or knowing how to keep it together. I was angry with her. I felt like an adult because I could see how messed up that was. Her behavior distorted my way of thinking about good and evil. As much as I loved her, I also hated her. Although I would never steal again, it proved more difficult to stop hating her.

By now, you know I had to take my hatred, pain and dislike for the man who was my pastor to the cross. After the Lord saved me, I didn't want anything stopping me from receiving the Holy Ghost. I had to take my mom to the cross. This didn't come easy. When I turned 15, her boyfriend came up to my bedroom. When I told my mother, she didn't respond, so I left the house that day and fortunately never returned. Mom asked Robert, "Why does she act that way toward me?" Robert told her why. The night or early morning her boyfriend came to my room I had a dream right before he was standing over me that he was standing over me, and then I awakened. I was calm and decided I would act like I was coming back to bed by saying I needed to use the bathroom. I'd rehearsed this plan in my head just in case my instincts were right; I went downstairs and never came back to the room. When

I told my mother, I saw in her face that she wasn't going to protect me, so I got out of there that same morning. I ran to Ruby' s house 103rd Green, a block away. (5am) Oct 1972.

Sometimes, I don't feel like I should have been saved by the Holy Ghost, but I am, and I know that God awakened me before this man could ever touch me. I love you, Lord. I thank You. I certainly forgive her although she pretends she doesn't remember. Now, I am under the blood, I have taken all that stuff to Jesus. Robert stood up for me. He seems to understand me. Why mention it now? Because I am not the only one, and I want to show you that you can forgive and you can keep it moving. Don't give up. Mend the fences that you can. Tell yourself you can make it, and you will with Jesus on your side. You're going to make it, so, don't give up.

When I went through that terrible separation, (leading to divorce) at age 56, a week shy of my 57th birthday, it was Robert Jr. who came over and spent one day a week with me, telling me how proud he was of me. I started dating in February 2012 and closed that friendship June 2016. I should have done it a few months earlier when he told me he was going to marry someone else. But two weeks to the date before my friend married someone else, I saw him daily. I am not sorry because it was a good way to rid myself of him in my heart. He did a lot of handy work around the house, especially outside near the air conditioning unit. I am sure that I needed him as much as he needed me before we both moved on in separate directions. His pain from foolish mistakes and my pain from my foolish mistakes.

Sometime around the middle of 2012 I went to the hospital to see Robert; he was suffering from COPD. I prayed with him, and demanded the devil to leave him in Jesus' name and he did. Robert hadn't smoked in years, but his common law wife did and second-hand smoke can be just as detrimental as smoking the cigarettes yourself. When I first started dating after 31 years of marriage, my brother was happy that someone else was cutting my grass. I hoped for a future, but God knows it was only for a space of time and for that season. I have taken this to the cross and I am letting go, in stages. He was my brother and my friend and I loved him. We seemed to share and help each other although some things in his life was hidden from me.

I wish I could see my brother now and hug him and give him water, but I can't. I have to accept what I have left and I have to remember that little boy calling me, Bebba. You can breathe now right, Brother? You are not subjected to this finite place. You don't have to worry anymore about your benefits. You don't have to worry about anymore back pay, or how you will get around with that oxygen tank, or how to use that inhaler. Did you leave on purpose? Because you had that inhaler on you that day but you didn't use it. You called me a few days before Thanksgiving. Did you know then? You almost fooled me and I tried to call you. I know you loved me. You were leaving this world and you were with Ivan and that's the way you wanted to do it. I told you, before you died, but I want to say it again you were so street smart. You had a lot of wisdom about the world and about life. Somehow, you and God had a talk and then you were gone. I was fixing the house because I didn't know if one day you were going to live with me and needed me, "Bebba," to give you some water. I sang a song, Drink from this water and you never thirst again...I play that song "I will never thirst again."

Robert, Bobby, you will never thirst again. Your last hour on earth, when your phone was ringing, your fiancée, dad and sister knew something was wrong. When it got to me, the voice mails said, "The voice mailbox belonging to ---is full and cannot receive messages at this time"; 45 minutes later Robert's transition had been finalized.

I am letting go, but in stages. His voice mailbox had never been full before and made me think something was different. I could feel it. I tossed that night. I didn't sleep well. The previous Thanksgiving, Robert did the Thanksgiving prayer. I asked God that morning when I awakened, who was going to do it this year? I didn't know, but I knew something had happened. I was on vacation at the time. On my way back from Nashville, I remember passing through Gary, Indiana and I cut the radio off as I headed into the home stretch. I could hear the Holy Ghost say, "You know things won't be the same after this year." I understood what that meant and I replied, "Yes, Lord". But I understood that the Lord was letting me know I was going to see 2017. Father never shared with me that I would see another year. I didn't know it was Robert, but I knew something was going to be different.

Remember all those gifts you brought us right after you got your 401k from that one job up North? The best Christmas we ever had; I bought you cologne. You bought all the boys' toys. Willie got a sweater and so did I. The gifts were beautiful, and I was amazed that you had such good taste and such a heart and desire to give to us. I will never forget that. Thank you, again, Robert, for being my brother and for loving me the way you did. Love always, "Bebba"

CHAPTER 8

My Wonderful Mother

I remember saying to my mom one Sunday evening when she called, "I know that you are tired and weary and you want something more out of life." Her cousin, sister Spencer would always say, "If Darlene ever gets saved, the devil will be losing someone who will do damage to his kingdom." When I was little, one of the colors I noticed that I thought was pretty on my mom was Kelly green. She wore it well and she had some of the nicest shoes and those first lady type hats were very nice. When my brothers and I were playing and goofing around we would hide in her closet and sit on the clothes and hats. Needless to say, I got the beating for it. I tried to keep things intact so I wouldn't keep getting those beatings. Some of the problem was that I would try on her clothes trying to be Ms. Grown-up. Eventually that played out and I let that go. You might say it was time to keep it moving.

Mom was a real vivacious personality but she was also wanting her way although she and dad didn't fuss much, he ruled and super ruled. She wasn't the kind of lady that allowed him to walk all over her and when she didn't get her way, she got her way anyway. He loved her very much and tried to stay prudent with the finances. She splurged frequently not concerned about the consequences of her actions when it came to spending. She spent money on us for clothes, food and junk food too. She took time from her busy work day as a currency exchange cashier and then manager, to take us to the museums and to Fun Town. Dad took us to Fun Town too and sometimes, we would go as a family. Dad didn't really want Mom to work but there was a cash shortage. She wanted here family to have more than enough, she wanted plenty. One might say, she was use to it.

She would complain that she didn't have enough to do what she wanted to do, and he would complain, that we couldn't live above our means. Either way, sometimes he would do what she wanted and give her what she wanted and then would close the wallet. She went along with that for a while but when she felt like his money wasn't cutting it, guess what? She was back working again. Working to make sure we had some of the finer thing in life, good clothes and toys. As kids, we tried to reward her by keeping the house clean. I think we did pretty good, but it failed in comparison to when she cleaned and cooked. I remember coming home on summer afternoons and smelling some good fried chicken, sweet potatoes and greens or cabbage and corn bread. It shall not be forgotten.

The pastor's wife made better cakes, but she did learn to make a cake that would pass the test. She allowed all the Sunday School kids to come to our house and although I really did not like the crowds, she was the Sunday School teacher. I guess you can say she proved to us all that she cared for the Christian education of the church children. We had sewing and embroidery classes, which were taught by a very nice lady; they were fun and I felt accomplished. Her name was Sister Bedford and she did not reminded me of my grandmother. My maternal grandmother didn't look like the average grandmother, she had swag. She made her cakes from Betty Crocker, and even though they were "box cakes", what was special about them was that she would put real bananas on the cake and add icing that made it delicious. Mother began to cry and I told her then that Jesus loves her and that He was waiting for her to come to Him to wash and cleanse her of all her sins. I explained to her that she would feel a burden lifted off of her shoulders once she gave her life to Him. She had lost her son while being a good mother, she and dad had. His name was Delbert; he lived to be maybe a month old. (early 60's)

After she was separated from Dad and thought she was going to marry the pastor, she had another son and his name was Marcellus. He was adopted and they renamed him Mark. Dad hoped for her to come back with all the phone calls between him and my grandmother, but that was far from her mind.

The pastor never stopped giving, either. He took my grandmother out for dinner with him and mom and she enjoyed the lavish treatments. But that didn't change anything; this was about to be a holy mess, but the years passed. Although life was never the same it didn't matter, Mom wasn't going to just fold up and die. She changed from the nice Sunday School teacher and just did what she wanted to do. Mom's lifestyle changed as a result of the man not leaving is wife. She had an affair and thought that he would, but he didn't. That made her change from nice to painfully irritated.

I explained further to Mom on the phone that we all have sinned and fallen short of the glory of God, but that once you are baptized in Jesus' name, you will notice the difference. Being filled with the gift of the Holy Ghost would seal her relationship with God and she would become a witness to tell others how to live and love Christ too. She received my soft message to her and I heard her say, "Okay, I will go to church near me and get baptized in Jesus' name".

It was fall and that Friday she went to Pastor Sudan's church and was baptized. I was told she came up from the water speaking in tongues. I was so happy for her and it was quite an experience. I had to forgive her for everything. Forgive her for what? Leaving our family committing adultery, putting other kid (who didn't have a mom) before me, and the abuse. I had to recognize that she is and always has been God's child.

Some time after that, I believe the pastor died. I decided not to go to the funeral. Although I forgave him for breaking up our family, I felt it was important to respect his wife and not attend. Although the church made him step down, he continued in a wayward way, (brought out at the funeral). So, I didn't go and it was a good decision for me; I do not regret that decision even to this day. I hope God forgave him for all the other things he had done too. I refuse to mention it because it's not what Christians should do; it's not how Christians should act.

Some of the good things he has done outweighed my anger and hatred I had for him. Besides, after I got saved, I made my peace with him and his wife. Mother seemed to enjoy her new life, saved. I appreciated all that my mom has gone through and when she finally landed a good job before getting saved, she met and married her third husband. They were really madly in love and although I didn't like it, I must admit they were in love, and they seemed to fit. Although he wasn't the pastor or church brother type, he was tall and brown and smooth unlike Mr. Jackson. I didn't get an opportunity to get to know this man because he died within two years of their marriage. I was with Mom during that process. She was a trooper and put him away well.

I wasn't happy with how she had to stand up to the family and deal with the insurance issues, but she made it through all that. The calling card for this love affair to me was that she had a life time bus pass to go anywhere in the United States as long as Greyhound traveled there. We never know where life will take us, but we must be receptive. She gets a widows social security, from being married. We must be forgiving and we must expect miracles to survive the storm tides of life.

My mom, Darlene, is eighty years old this year. I suspect she will live a long time and she still has the get up and go power and the Lord has been with her. She lost her son last year, her protector and seems to be dealing with it very well. I don't see her slowing down anytime soon. She is very active at our church and is accepted among the church family. She was very supportive when my ex-husband left me and showed kindness when I was in need reminding me of the many times, I gave her money, unexpectedly. She is brave, strong and able to make it through anything. She is the "Unsinkable Molly Brown", one of the movies we watched together when I was a little girl.

It was a movie we would watch together on some nights when we were a family. She would come in my room and get in bed with me and eat popcorn. Dad was at work and the boys were sleep. A mothers' love cannot be replaced and so I give you flowers my darling mother, who bore the pain of caring me nine months. Allowing me to live and caring for me the best you knew how. I forgive you for breaking us up and even if I didn't, God did. He has thrown all your faults in the sea of forgetfulness. Run free dear, laugh and love, for you have earned your place in this world. You have paid a great price and now you can lay your crown at the feet of Jesus. My mother, my friend, my mother, my love. As for forgiving you, I am able to keep it moving.

CHAPTER 9

Something Within

Have you ever heard the statement, *Something within me that holdeth the rain?* I don't know if that is a baby boomer, religious parent statement, religious saying, church pastor preaching saying, all I know is that it is true. Something within me that holdeth the rain. Life has a way of showing you just what part you are playing. Can you change that part? Yes. You can become almost anything and everything you want to be. I say that because so many years while being married, I wanted to take a cruise. I didn't go on a cruise because the man I was married to would not take me and down talked ever wanting to plan a cruise. But this year, the year that I graduate with my MBA, I am taking a boat cruise. This vacation is my gift to myself for putting in the time, meeting new people, professors and other educators and peers, all of them helped me, in changing my part.

Something within me that holdeth the rain. What does that mean? It means no matter what is going on, you have learned to balance your life around or end the storm. No matter how the blows come. Which include disappointments, being betrayed, or finding out the man or woman you love doesn't love you, and yet, something within you holdeth the rain. If you are like me, you know that something, is knowing that God is going to send the sun. You know no matter how dark the night, the joy of the Lord will be your strength. You know that if you have someone to support you, and have become your support system, you know you are blesse, and that God put these people in your life, and that you are to be a point of inspiration for someone too. Look at The Fair Well of Bobby Jones Gospel. I really thank God for his sacrifice to bring us beautiful gospel artists for 35 years. I hope we find him doing something else because I appreciate what he has given us. I saw Kirk Franklin give the tribute. I remember meeting Kirk Franklin. I should have asked him to take me under his wings then. But I also realized I was working this department (CPD) and I was committed to finishing this career. I certainly hope I get an opportunity to meet Kirk Franklin again. I had an opportunity to meet Bobby Jones for his birthday celebration when Nathan from Nashville worked on some of my music, where he "Nathanized" it. But after recording all day and realizing I had to preach in Knoxville in a day or so, I figured I better try to recover, plus I was traveling with my grandchildren, mom, and son, William. I thought I better stay put, but I know that would have been wonderful. That CD is called "I Played That Song"; singing certainly help build faith and hope in the Lord. I appreciate fellowshipping with the Lord through song as well as deliberating on His holy word.

I know that something within me holdeth the rain. I don't really know what the author or the individual was thinking about when they pinned the phrase, song or saying. But this I know – they must have felt, like I do, that Jesus and His word and the works of His had in our lives was holding the rain. Holding the tears from getting so out of control that we could not stop crying. Holding the rain, when we lost our job, when our family members were killed, or in a car accident, or a family member was raped, or even ourselves treated unjustly and not to forget during slavery years. Our ancestors had to know that it was something within, after being so far from home brought their culture from Africa to the United States. When men were shipped off from place to place to make babies, to make more slaves; when women and girls were used for the pleasure of the slave master, there was something that holdeth the rain.

I sometimes watch how I sleep, and I note my mannerism. I note my attitude when I am the only black person in the room. I note when I hear them talking about me. But there is something within me that holdeth the rain.

It is hard sometimes to see slavery in slow motion even after the cotton gin. After Jim Crow, after separate but equal, after affirmative action. After the flood of other nations of immigrants who are certainly getting many opportunities that African Americans fought for. With many others and with white people who put down their funds and education and law degrees and their lives for the sake of justice, something within me that holdeth the rain. I unfortunately, am reminded of hatred and bigotry and how we are always the first to go to the back of the bus.

How does slavery get to live and breathe in our communities? Through drugs. How do drugs live in our communities? By liquor and grocery stores, and by people who are aware of the plan to keep this community and race of people down. Selling open cigarettes, and liquor in cups "trap that black man – young and old fall into it." Something within me that holdeth the rain. Slavery: when we look at movies and television that shows the crime and no drawing the line. Programming that looks to demoralize black women and men and show most blacks living in swallow and waste. I am almost done with my MBA program. Even there, this sense of, *why is this old lady getting a degree?* exists. Would it be alright if I were white, Indian, or from another race? Something within me that holdeth the rain. I wish we could love and not have discrimination. One group, one race, one people, one gang, one way of thinking; no one thinking they are better than the next. I understand that there are bad people in every race. Some need a chance to change and that opportunity is hard to find. I want to cry sometimes, and sometimes I do when I think about what harm drugs can do. I cry sometimes when I think about how hard it is for a black man to be able to step out of the stereotype that (all he's good for) is sleeping around and being lazy. In reality, there are many barriers standing in his way, and he gives up easy and quick, or traps are set he can't even see coming. If he goes to school and try hard to be something, he better not come back to the hood because somebody might just take him out. Something within me that holdeth the rain.

CHAPTER 10

I See It Now

―――――○―――――

It was a glorious day; the sun was shining so bright and I was feeling as if I was at the top of my game. Did I really have game or was I in my flesh? Whatever it was, I was in love.

I loved working in the yard; the flowers were beautiful and he could cut the grass. I would cook the meal (lunch or dinner) sometimes both. Oh, I see it now, but not then; I needed him and he needed me. After going through such a put down and the husband walking away asking to come back after telling me what he did, I said no. Was I just hurt? I don't really know. I was so happily distracted from my cares and worries. I was not really interested in anything at the time except being a good friend, a friend who wanted my friend to know that I love Jesus and planned to live out the rest of my life in obedience. I can't tell you that he wanted what was best for me; I can't say I was looking out for his best interest either. I couldn't see then, but I see it now.

I think at times we were trying to keep Christ first. I think at times we needed a human person to care about our pain and to say it will be alright. By that time, rumors were flying and our friendship became something else in the eyes of our friends. People who didn't care for him were looking for a reason to keep the rumors alive knowing they were not true. I wish they would have just let it be, instead of making something good, become bad and ugly. We were not thinking that way at all. It was something special and rare and then it went to another place. We pressed beyond the rumors and because we both needed someone, we stuck it out until we were to stand alone. No one told me about his reputation. I probably would not have believed them and yes, I ignored the rumor. I ignored the things that were being said over the phone for about a year. He denied it at first, but I see it now. My brother, my friend, was truly my friend I thought, or was he just self-serving, self-surviving? All is fair in love and war.

Once everything caught up to him, he said. "I knew if I told you the truth, you would not have gone out with me. "You think"? There is no excuse for being stupid or blind. Was it really love? I hope so. I hope he shall never forget me, because I meant him well. I pray for his life, his marriage to be good. I hope happiness and joy will carry him through his old age. I used to enjoy the bible classes we had together. He was like my private pastor back then. I would sing him some of my new songs. It's what we did.

Took a cruise to the West Caribbean Ocean as a graduation gift to myself. It was well worth it. The trip reminded me that I am moving on. I am so glad, because without God's help, it would have been challenging to move on. I kept feeling like he wanted to just keep on being whatever we were. But my God moved in me and my righteous indignation arose. I gathered enough strength from my faith in the living God to tell him, "Just like you moved on, allow me to do the same." He said "I saved you." I then said, "I know, I dodged the bullet."

I know how he thinks, and feels about life, and the low self-esteem he has about himself and struggling to keep up, but that's her business not mine. That's why I said, don't call me anymore, I don't need anybody else's baggage. I'm done, too. I'm moving on. I'm blessed to have God who cares about me. I don't have to deal with that issue anymore. I can keep it moving. I couldn't see it then, but I see it now. I needed to feel special and he fulfilled that void in my life. He needed to feel he could love again. (The way God planned it)

Apparently in the back of his mind, he had a tender heart for his now wife. I am glad; I could be of some help to my brother, my friend. My love, who is no longer mine to mention. I am not sorry and I am not disappointed. To my surprise, I have been left feeling so fulfilled and so complete. How is that possible, that I don't feel betrayed?

What God has for me is for me and he was only a loan for a very short space of four years. Take it or leave it. I choose to keep it moving. In the book of Galatians 5:1 (KJV), it says, "Stand fast therefore in the liberty wherewith Christ hath made us free and be not entangled again with the yoke of bondage." When your assignment is over in someone's life, pick yourself up and keep it moving. You are worth the move. You are worth the thunder of living. You are worth the sprinkling of God blood over your entire being, Body, Mind, and Soul.

God's word clearly tells us not to be entangled again, which means it is quite possible that we will be entangled at some point in our lives. Let us seek the will God has for our lives and not allow anyone to stigmatize us and put their spin on our relationships. It may be hard or difficult to be in a relationship with the opposite sex and other times it isn't, but stand on that. We can't pick who we are to minister to; we can't discriminate on who God will use to help us from a place of incomprehensibility. Helping another person, should be honored and not disannulled as taboo. Everyone you meet may not be in your life forever, but for a space of time so that you can impart to one another what each of you may need in order to meet your next challenge. Don't allow anyone to take your good and change it into something revolting and unclean. I wish we were not willing to gossip and try to make something out of innocence to be wrong or force people with our lips to be more than what they are capable of being to one another. I would sing hymns, and I gave him a hymn book because you can draw strength from those songs.

I am better for knowing him. He may have been one way around others, but with me he was fun, funny and gave me emotional shelter. We viewed politics alike. My buddy, my friend, I too am moving on. He was sometimes confused, sometimes too nice, and sometimes unable to say no. I found him to be compassionate and gentle toward me. I was able to help him decide, to try to love again. I guess it worked.

If not me, someone. He was my friend and needed me as much as I needed him. I am stronger for it, that he told me he was moving on, and I was stuck. I called on the Lord with tears and more tears I didn't see it then. I thought for sure we would be together forever. So, I keep it moving. It's over now and I am better for it. Instantly I knew God wanted more for me, I just had get pass this carnal block, I see it now.

But somehow, some way, I was able to muster up some strength, to tell him, since he was now married, to let me go, and let me move on too, just as he had done. January 2, 2017, sometime in the afternoon, I felt empowered after making that sane decision. I love holiness, and sanctification, and had no intentions of being stupid at this eye-opening stage of life.

He always said he wanted more for me, than himself. "Your husband is going to buy you a big house" Maybe he really was not enough for me. I didn't care that he had little or nothing. I am happy now that God was looking out for me, giving me nothing of what I wanted and making sure I only have what I need. I need God. I need God's continual support and I needed to be like my father. To hear him when he calls, when he talks to me, and when he walks through the house. (my home)

I didn't see it then, but I see it now. This was said to the bitter end, he was not enough for me, and I deserved more. Perhaps, he was right. His friends posted pictures. I was in total disbelief, but then I got used to the idea. I see it now. Moving on, keeping it moving was what I had to do. Keeping it moving, still praying and fasting feeling so complete, satisfied and fulfilled once again. I'm now doing well. I feel better about letting go. I'm keeping it moving, It is never to late to ask father for his help, when you are blindsided wounded in intense battle, or ambushed.

Moving on the ocean so far away from home, standing on the balcony, listening to the ocean waves, smelling the ocean air, and glad to be alone learning who I am as a survivor of love gone wrong. Learning who I am as a woman destined for God's favor, graduating with a Masters degree in Business Administration. Empowered by opposition and grace from above. God smiling down on me; I may not deserve His care. God cares for me and I am so glad He does. This amazing love has given me a kinder, softer way, and I am more willing to show compassion to others, as Christ has shown to me. So now less willing to be "Holier than thou" It must be holiess from God, not of ourselves.

I didn't see it then, but I see it now. My life is hidden in Christ. Otherwise, people would drive you in a direction you had no intentions of going. Keep it moving, lift your chin little children. Run and play and let God know you love Him and He will protect you from the wolves. He shall guide you in a planned path.

Father is the good Shepherd. He lays in the sheepfold, so that no one can come into the door without His approval. No one can threaten your soul or salvation without him knowing about it. He will not allow the enemy to prey over you to destroy the work He has done in you. Cleaning you up, making you meat for the masters use and to sit at his table. Don't allow anyone to judge you on the basis of their lack of understanding of human need for consolation and honest warmth from another human being. God has a messenger for you, to support and restore you, for His own use. Do we support people because we want to? Sometimes. Should we discriminate against who should receive our help? No. But we still do, although it doesn't make it right.

So, as we pass through life, remember you may be someone's comfort; you may be someone's hope. You may teach or learn to keep it moving, and to let go, so that individuals can learn to fly again. Stand down with your words of cruelty, and show compassion for the gospel sake, but keep it moving.

CHAPTER 11

The Final Chapter

---○---

The Lord woke me up this morning around 5:00 am. I felt rested and I got up slowly walking throughout the house praying softly being thankful for another day while putting on the coffee. I continued to walk throughout the house asking God's blessing on little Khloe, Kenster Jr., Kenster and India, my son and daughter-in-law. I then prayed for Josh and his daughter, Samaura, her brother "Daddy Man" and their mother, Crystal. I then turned attention to William and Jerade, his son Jerade Jr., Brianna and Riniah and their mother. (Brody).

Although he tells me stories about his ex-wife, I will not allow that to stop me from praying for my grands and for their mother, my ex daughter-in-law. I miss her being a part of my life, but sometimes when it's over, it's just over. It's up to the two of them to keep their family glued together after a divorce, of which I know so well. It's hard work either way so you might as well stay married and work it out. Just like the weather, sometimes we just like to complain – it's too warm or it's not warm enough. When will it stop raining?

Several days have passed and at least a week or two until graduation. I have two last classes to take and God knows I am really feeling the pressure from being in the classroom and taking tests, and learning new things and new ideas. I have reached my limit for learning things outside of my gifted area, which is Theology, Divinity, Romans and Biblical Studies. I feel a sense of relief that I have come this far and now it's really almost over. I may consider enrolling in the Doctoral program from the Dr. D.R. Bell Bible College, which is now accredited. I did my first bachelors degrees there and finished in 1995, 1996. The first in Religious Services and second in ministry.

I remember the 1990's and early 2000's teaching at the bible college. I appreciate Dr. Sullivan allowing me to teach bible survey. Bishop Moore allowed me to teach his classes and Bishop Bell allowing me to teach Romans 1 and 3; the late Bishop Wright would allow me to teach Romans 3. Bishop Bellamy would let me substitute for him. There were so many classes and so much to learn about scripture, doctrine, the history of the church. Bishop Price would always describe his history class as "Hi Story" the person who tells a story that becomes history. I certainly can't forget Evangelist Robinson and her Husband Elder Robinson. The most profound teacher was my good friend, who was also like a good grandmother, Mother Mary Frances Pebbles. She was our Minister Alliance Chair, for the Christ Temple Apostolic Faith Church. She was my homiletics' instructor, and yes, she allowed me to sub for her as well. I thank God for those days. I will see them all again, although a few of the professors, instructors are still supporting and teaching at the bible college and keeping the doors open.

Fortunately, I was able to go to church on Mother's Day. I cried little tears during the service, as I felt my soul being purged and the Holy Spirit washing me, and helping me to stay tender and gentle, and for that I was so grateful. I feel that my church is one of the most dynamic churches in this city. I appreciate the service of each person from hospitality to the choir singing and the effort the ministries used, especially our pastor, when preaching the morning sermon. I want to stay for both services and soak it all in, but I am still working nights and sometimes I rush home to take a shower and then off to church. I know the day is coming when I can stay in service, eat at church and leave when the lights go out and serve in some form and capacity, like when I first became a member. During the years my bishop was still living. I once sang in the choir, dismissed service, prayed and served communion. I don't know where the strength came from and at that time, I was working the street as a relief cop to the beat officers, until I got my own beat, at the park district. That was helpful and my life became much easier to manage and I was "Officer Friendly." With Saturdays and Sundays off, it was blissful. I loved Sundays then and I love Sundays now.

The final chapter represents, "I can do all things through Christ which strengthens me." I am single and it feels good. I am abstaining and it feels good. The Lord has supplied all my needs according to his riches in glory to Christ Jesus. I am a conquer. The final chapter is a portfolio of the past 6 years. The final chapter is really finding out what type of woman I am. To my own hurt, I was able to say I refuse to be second. I refuse to go against God's covenant laws. I refuse to be on bad terms with my moral and ethical core. I refuse to frustrate the gospel of Christ down in my soul, down deep in my soul.

The final chapter says I deserve better. The final chapter tells me that I have arrived. Oh, not with houses, land, fine clothes, jewelry or hitting the lottery. But I have arrived in the sense that I do not want to make God angry, and I have no reason to doubt His power in my life. I am anxious for nothing, but by prayer and supplications, I will continue to make my request known to God. Our God reigns and He reigns from heaven above with wisdom, power, and love. God is an Awesome God.

The final chapter is deep clarification for me that God doesn't leave His creation, that He does desire to fellowship with His loved ones and He will go to an extreme to have a relationship with you. He will move heaven and earth into hell to find you. It was David who said If I make my bed in hell, thou art there. You and I can not hide from Father, otherwise we will hear him say: Debora-/_____ (your name) where art thou? Papa Jesus builds us up so we can stand on mountains.

Final Chapter show restraint not because there is none, but because what we may want is not good for us. It can cause us to fall short of the real plan and the real blessings He has laid up for us. For eyes have not seen, nor ear heard of the things that the Lord hath in store for them that love him. The final chapter assures me I have options. I have a God who really loves me. I have capabilities and capacity to gain and retain. Not of my own, but what he has equipped me with.

Final chapter invites God's plan for my life into my life. I hear Aretha Franklin singing in my final chapter, "My soul looks back and wonder how I got over." Final chapter is about a girl who became a woman who has learned to take the bitter with the sweet. For all is fair in love and war, and the weapons of our warfare are not carnal. It's not against a man or a woman, but against my will to please God, and to love pleasing Him and to love adoring and serving Him. That is what the enemy is fighting. He doesn't want us to give God, his Glory by magnifying him with a sanctified life. But he deserves the Glory, He deserves my praise. My new CD release is called, *All of Me*. Final chapter is about making sure I have put no other god before my God. No matter how tempting and delicious it appears, but it is a cloak of a wolf in sheep's clothing. No matter how soft and tender his touch, run. Run like "Forest Gump" ran. Because he means you no good. She means you no good.

Let us pray: May God's peace rise over your flock. May we recognize the sheepfold is maintained by you, and we need not fear. For if any man comes up any other way besides coming through the sheepfold where our Lord is, is a thief and a robber. I dare not trust the sweetest frame. But wholly and whole heartily lean on Jesus' name. On Christ the solid rock I stand, all other ground is sinking sand. In Jesus Name Amen.

CHAPTER 12

Keep It Moving

———————○———————

You have been praying a long time. One son is healed and another one is doing some substance, and drinking now, and it's out of control, that is what his fiance said, and when he comes around, he certainly has been performing that way. He is not the young man I know. What can I do about it? It's time to pray. I wasn't really expecting this because it took a lot of time and energy and prayer and tears to pray the other one through and asking the saints to pray with me. I don't blame any of the kids for our divorce, but I can truly say that it certainly can bring you to a place of trial.

When a child is sick or dying or doing drugs and disrupts the flow of the family, your marriage can and will be tested. Did I see it coming? No, but I knew it was possible as I call each of their names out. I guess that's why he's been calling me weekly and now daily because he's in trouble. I'm his mom and he expects for me to fix it. But since I have a regular prayer time and relationship with Father, I know this trial isn't for me to get close to the Lord, this young man is 35-years-old, we are telling Satan to stand down because he belongs to the Lord. We decree it and claim him for the Lord. I will not waiver; we claim the victory over this demonic strong hold. In Jesus' name.

Father hear my cry and answer me speedily. Please do not let the enemy have his way with Josh. This is a warning, and my son wants me to tell him that if he doesn't... but I am not going to say it. I will pray for him, to my surprise he is afraid to make the change. He is being what he isn't and it's showtime. He has to choose the devil and hell or Jesus and Heaven. His speech sounds as if he is attacking me and I am now made aware that since I am in convenant relationship with Jesus, he's attacking me. He is angry that both God and the devil are fighting for him. He will not be able to stand, still he will need to move forward by faith or by letting the devil lead him down the path of no return, God forbid. Josh is taking it out on me. But when we hear God's voice, we should not harden our hearts (Psalms 95:8). When he came up for Mother's Day, I could not tell him right away, but it was brewing. It was happening. I couldn't get him to rest. He left out to be with people that really could hurt him. But they didn't and I am grateful. God is still holding him and covering him in His precious blood.

My oldest spent a few hours with him too. It seems to hurt him as he told me about his younger brothers' action. (Josh), Josh grew up in holiness and he knows what he has been running from for a long time. He may have been playing like he had the Holy Ghost, but my boy, William really did get it. Now that God has healed him, he is ready to face reality again. William leans on me, but he's not heavy. He's my boy. He is better and he is coming along very well. He spends the night and we have a set date, for him to come home for good. Right at the time God has given us victory and given him strength to face reality. He is frightened too, but he has come a long way and he wants all the benefits of being in the family. His brother is dealing with the same ungodly issues because he himself has been through so much.

I was expecting that he would have learned from his mistakes, and was moving on. (Josh) I figured because he was older, he had learned from his past mistakes. Saved or not, there should come a time when you realize this isn't working for me and I am to old for these games. But when one is angry with the structure, that may not be reasonable and paying your dues to society may bring more pressure than you bargain for, it can keep you from gasping the theme, "Keep It moving". When one is desperate and voracious for living right, you will change; you will make a decision. I just hope his decision will be one of progress, hope and investment in eternal life instead of eternal damnation. I want to see Josh in heaven. I want to see all of are children in heaven. I want to see his face here on earth, in peace, I want to see your children in peace. I want him to outlive me and watch his daughter turn into a little preacher lady. I love her and to my surprise, she is a lot like me. Her mom Crystal's confirms that.

Today is Crystal's birthday and I already told her I would send her something. Josh please hear God's voice and come forth in victory. You may be in the fight of your life and I hope you choose life, instead of growing and going forward, he is pacing, he is irritated and he is afraid. Afraid of himself and afraid to progress; afraid that if he puts forth an effort, he might just like it. He is moping instead of looking up; he mopes but he needs to learn to keep it moving. Education is something you really have to desire. Right now, he is frustrating me and his family. Why? Because he is crying out for help in his own way. Instead of my son giving in, give it up to God the Father. He's able to bring you out. Cry out to God. Put not your trust in man, money, gambling, smoking, doping, drinking, card playing. Give God the issues of your life. You don't like who you are? Change it son.

God is the one who holds the keys to death, hell, and the grave. God is the one who can give you new life and bring you into the kingdom of His dear Son. He is more than able to bring you out. He will give you an inheritance among them that are sanctified. Cast your cares on Him, my son, and wait on the Father for he can give you peace even after I have left this earth. But he would not listen when we tried to help him. He went his own way and made himself his parents.

The Josh Prayer

Now father we/his family are once again coming before you on behalf of Josh, asking that you would have mercy on him and remove the taste for drugs and alcohol out of his life. Come inside and fill him with your love and power, and cleanse him from all iniquity. You know because he is not talking right, he isn't listening and father he can't hear your voice because he is drowning it out with drinking and clubbing. He said he doesn't, but its not looking good, but father you can turn it around and it's not over for Josh until you say its over. Please let my son live not survive, not shake or bake, but live a holy life. I decree it, I stand proxy for other mothers and fathers for the healing of their sons and daughters too, and count it as done, in Jesus' name, Amen.

You just finished a mission in your own personal life, but not without a cost. Burning the midnight oil, dealing with rejection from a relationship, learning to live single and abstinent. Preparing for retirement, in the middle of all this, I lost it. I engaged in an argument about a seat in God's house. She pointed her finger in my face and said it's on you, she refused to forgive me, and I decided to forgive her, I walked into that one, it was my fault it was a battle I didn't need to fight. I was not able to convince the person that I was talking to that I sit there every Sunday, and technically, she was right. She didn't have to care. She didn't care, I should not have cared and this is far more damaging and more difficult to fight. "But God" every Sunday for almost 15 years now, that is where I sit, but it didn't go well and there was nowhere to turn except find a new seat. I take the blame for that mishap because I had a vision earlier in the week where to sit, but I ignored that idea once I went to church and was engaged in Sunday School. I was trying to reconcile, but she was trying to keep the blame on me. Wow, so unlike my idea to love. I never expected to fall into that trap. It was easy to see another person's mistake, but on the same token, I should have been willing to give up my seat without the hassle of trying to defend myself.

When I look at the situation, it is only pride. Even if I was being thrown out with the bath water, I shouldn't care, I should have let that go. I will keep it moving and learn from that misfortune. I realize teeth and tongue fall out, but love is patient, and kind and we can never expect someone to understand our logic, but they can understand our love, they will know us as Christians by our love. Even if they don't say it, they will understand you didn't retaliate. I was misunderstood and there was no turning back. No matter what I said, this sister was going to blame me no matter what and take no responsibility. Rightfully so, I should have been silent. This was not a teachable moment. Or was it? Lord I repent. This was a trap from the enemy to steal my joy while going through this episode with another kid.

How long will this take? My life is far spent and the day is at hand. I know this story too well, Josh went by to see William, left him clothing and some of his finer jewelry. As a nurse, this isn't a good sign. He is either preparing to go back to jail or something worse, but we can't stay there we must believe that God will make all things beautiful in His time. I must have faith and believe that God will heal Josh from his sickness, his sin and that he too will be delivered, and set free. *God is able to do just what He said He would do. Don't give up on God because he wants give up on you... He's able.* I will supplicate. I will pray daily and out to papa Jesus for his help.

"Lord here I am again this time, again on behalf of Josh. I am so sad for him. I'm so sorry for how he is beaten down by Satan. Please father give him another chance to get it right."

I may be looking at this from a rational perspective and may not be able to see the dysfunctions of this situation that is going up against our family once again. I could feel it in the atmosphere, when early Sunday morning I awakened from a good night's sleep that I truly was going to need that strength to keep it moving. I walked through the house praying for each of my children, and around 5:20 am the doorbell rang. I knew it was Josh, but what I didn't know is he didn't seem like himself. He left out abruptly almost like a mad man. But something was holding him, preventing him from hurting me, preventing him from total destruction. I realized my boy was another baby in trouble. After seeing what God had done for Mr. William, I am convinced my son is in trouble and intercessory prayer is a must. With all the awful things going on in jails and encounters with the police, and the fact he has young daughter, depending on him, to get it right this time. It's not working. His dad was leaving him his summer home.

But under the circumstances I suggested he put the deed in trust under Josh's daughter's name, our granddaughter, because of what we are facing with him. I have heard my granddaughter quote scripture and I have seen my granddaughter's excitement for church and for the things of our Lord. I am happy about that, but right now, her father is in need and I have to stand proxy for him. Do you need to stand proxy for someone in your family as well? Let's keep it moving and bombard heaven for them. Father will hear us. Josh went back to jail, on traffic issues in received his GED. Thank you Lord, continue to help mothers and fathers everywhere.

Being Strong

I'm tired Father, and I really don't want to do this again. I spent so much energy and time praying and I remember in December 2006 when I gave William to you. Now, its May 2017, and I could see it on his face, hear it in his voice. He drove all the way from Tennessee just to say Happy Mother's Day or to make me think that I should not be happy or to show me how messed up he is. Although I wanted to see the Josh I have known in and out of jail and working one fast food to the next, alongside his family and yet now it's no longer in unity; it's sporadic and unpredictable. You can't hide this. It stands out like a sore thumb. It's a problem. It's a enormous. It's an elephant in the room.

When Josh stormed out the house on Mother's Day, I wasn't sure if he was leaving town; this was around 5:30 am. I didn't offer to give him any money and he didn't ask. I went about my morning preparing for church and believed that my number 4 son was going to send him money to go home. The Lord woke me up Monday morning around

3:15 am; at 3:29 Josh called and because of the encounter I had with him on Mother's Day, there was no way I was going to have another one at least not that early. I asked if his brother sent him money to go home? He said yes or he didn't understand the question. I told him that he had left his clothing and he said he would like to come get them. I told him they would be on the porch in a plastic bag and that the clothing had been washed. He needed to understand that his behavior was not acceptable.

Once he came to get the clothing, I went back to sleep, but I didn't feel he had left town and I was right. I awakened around 8:45 am, which was pretty late for me, but having an encounter like that and praying, it can throw you; I'm not nearly able to handle the rough roads of life as I once did. My boys are all grown now except I am Mr. Williams' guardian and I guess the devil doesn't have anything else to work with so he used this son to remind me that he is in charge of this earth and the diabolical substances, ripping families apart. You might say here we go again, but I also say, what the bible says: "We wrestle not against flesh and blood, but against principalities and powers against the rulers of darkness, against spiritual wickedness in high places" (KJV).

I realize I must brace myself and put it all in the hands of Jesus. Every time Josh had an issue, we tried to fix it. He went through many cars. This last time, I gave him a car I purchased from Kenny, and India,to help and he didn't seem thankful for the car at all. He seems to want to pretend he has more that what he has. I wish he understood that his value is not in what you have, it's in Christ Jesus, our Lord. I can hear the songwriter, "I know you'll come through what steps should I take, what move should I make, oh Lord. I'm going to wait". I hope my boy will be quickening; Lord, I ask that you breathe life into Josh and let not the enemy destroy him or take him from this earth without you in his life the way he should know you. Listen for you, Love and trust you.

When I found Jesus it was wonderful. I don't know what it's like to grow up in holiness and have people surrounding you who really care for others for their salvation needs. But it amazes me that they had this training and opportunity and it passed them. Let it not be too late, dearest Lord. Those were days when they would tarry with you. I wish I could make him, or pour it inside of him to love and obey you, Lord. I am limited. You have all power. God will not leave us alone to fight these battles without his protection and care. Satan the Lord God reprimands you. You will not go undone sowing tares among the wheat. Keep it moving, Satan because the LORD has already planned your time left here on earth. Keep it moving, Satan, because God will not destroy the righteous with the wicked.

When our children have squandered time playing in a devil's world missing out on some the most profound moments in history, I repent for our sins, and encourage them to find a savior. Keep it moving when your heart is breaking and don't ever give up. Don't give up on loving, don't give up on hoping, and don't give up on believing. For God will open doors. Ask God for one more day, and keep it moving. Jesus, can I wash your feet? I know you must feel tired sometime. So, can I wash your feet?

Keep it moving saints, because God can do anything but fail. He can save, and he can heal, and according to His will, God can do anything but fail. It is not to late for Josh, let him go. Keep it moving Satan, not to another child, but find yourself to the place set aside for you and your angels who followed you from heaven doors. Keep it moving Satan to a place of utter darkness, away from the children of the highest. The fire is hot but not for the children and not for the children of men, but for you.

Declare Yourself

Declare yourself to be a child of God, and call on the name that is bigger and greater than any name, that at the name of Jesus, every knee shall bow, and every tongue shall confess, that Jesus Christ is Lord. Keep it moving. Night will turn directly into day. The sun will shine again, your heart will heal and your mind will be transformed and your soul will be revived. Tell yourself, parade this thought and carry the flag, Christ is the answer. Keep it moving when you're happy and keep it moving when your sad. Heaven is your home, until God gets ready to clean up this earth where eventually we shall live forever. Oh, we are coming back when Satan is defeated, so keep it moving.

Don't do it your way Josh, Satan take your hands off my child, and take your hands off the children of men making them your slaves to the captivity of drugs and crime and gangs and habitual habits of lust and greed and gambling and sickness and disease. Boys and girls, I know they want to teach you evolution, but you were created for God and for his glory. You were created in the image and likeness of Father, and not as the lower creatures that he made for your use. The lower creatures were for your amusement, for your friendship, and for you to control, not man controlling man, but man was made to love, and think like a Holy God. Keep it moving people find your place in Christ and fight for the right of that liberty, no longer a slave to sin and shame and degradation – not when Christ has set you free! Keep it moving when you don't have the answers to life, by faith call on the God of Heaven and earth. He has all the answers to your issues and He is full of wisdom and knowledge and understanding. He knows just what to do. Bring the chin up, and smile, because Christ is the answer!

You keep on after our homes, our husbands and wives, children, place of business and worship too; we got something for you. Down on our knees in prayer. We will fast and pray, and continue in supplication. Because we know who can get you off our backs and shoulders and we know who can keep you away from our minds and hearts. Get back Satan don't you come any further. You can attack my mind and body, but He keeps my soul. I wish I could pour this next scripture into the minds of our youth and in the minds of young men and women everywhere. Let me not forget to cling and hold on to this wisdom from scripture from Gods law.

"The law of the Lord is perfect, converting the soul: the testimony of the Lord is sure, making wise the simple. The statues of the Lord are right rejoicing the heart: the commandment of the Lord is pure enlightening the eyes."

Sin pays, but it isn't a nice salary. It brings and promises death, darkness and confusion. Choose life, choose ye this day whom you will serve (KJV). I realize there are no perfect people. But God is perfect and He gave us Jesus who knew know sin, and gave Himself and made Himself sin for us, that all of our stumbling in darkness is nailed to a cross called Calvary. So now I can live, as his blood covers me.

Hallelujah! From sin, shame and eternal death. When God looks at me, Mercy says, "See the blood on his/her shoulder. See the love instead of hate. See the healing instead of the wounds."

Part 2

He backed himself into a wall, he was confused and didn't know which way to go, and yet he already had made up his mind, to keep it moving. He went for council and the preacher told him, to keep it moving. I don't know if he is running, but he's too old to make mistakes now. You better make it count. No time to be stagnated man, just keep it moving.

He caught you at a vulnerable state. That's not his fault that's what he does and when he's finished with you, he will tell you we are back to where we started; it's a game to him. You should tell him you are keeping score, and he's lost points and he should keep it moving. Don't beat yourself up, just change your atmosphere. Repent and ask God for His leading and guidance through the forest and through the wilderness. I see you. You are better and you are walking upright before Father. Don't stop, keep it moving. When your time comes, you will know it, and you will be loved for who you are. When you're working hard to please the man, stop. It his job to make the big sacrifice, otherwise he will not appreciate you. But remember it's a two-way street, and once you both committed, work in harmony and unity well after the "I Dos". Keep it moving and keep your chin up.

The race is not given to the swift nor to the strong, but to him, that endure to the end. So, keep on holding on, hold to faith and hold on to

Jesus, don't ever let go. When you become thrilled over some of the wonders of life, do not forget, that Christ is always there for you, to pick you up from the falls and scrapes of life. He will be there for you with the first aid kit, with power and healing, to deliver you from the forces and terror of evil.

Find ways to be grateful, because someone else is worse off than you. Someone else would love to be in your shoes, even if they are unable to fill those shoes. Keep it moving and don't let go. Father has dispatched his angels to watch over you to encourage you, in his word, in song, or wherever you can get plugged in, to what is right, and good. Remember, God will take care of you, "So Keep it Moving."

That old devil set a trap for you, and you fell into it, but because you didn't do it willfully God delivered you. Because you were not into the intent, God allowed you to exit that trauma and that drama. Take your negative experience in life, for an example, let those experiences teach you humility, and softness and do not allow Satan to make you bitter. Let them laugh, but keep on moving in a positive direction.

Why are we so hard on others and often time too hard on ourselves as well? Regroup, rethink this thing you are experiencing, and refresh yourself with songs, hymns, prayer and deliberate compassion for yourself. Drench your soul in Gods ready word. Purge yourself from self-hate, and don't be disconcerted about who you are. You need this for your life because you have to keep it moving. Don't allow yourself to get stuck with how people view you. You have the right to be kind to yourself, and do not allow people to rain and walk through your parade without a positive contribution. Pray for them for they cannot see the full picture of who God is making you to be. Don't get angry, the sun is shining on you, "Let the sun do what it does."

Cried myself to sleep last night, so many moons ago, and boy I am so glad I did. What comfort that was to release what was inside of me. I am not a man, and even if a man cries, it's okay too. I would not think less of you because you cried. It's okay because you hurt too. It's okay you are black and you are a real man; they don't treat you like you are, and you must find a way to be declared, or you will explode. I will help you in any way that I can to uphold and encourage you, and believe in you black man, black boy, black child. I want and need your protection. Don't rape your women. Don't steal from them. Don't run from woman to woman, giving each of them venereal diseases. You are married, your wife is hurt because you brought it home to her, and she doesn't feel comfortable going to the doctor, when it's not her, it's you. I'm sorry but it's true, so get yourself together. She is willing to give you another chance to get it right. Faith has a great payment plan, It pays back for trusting and waiting and believing in the Father, Lord God almighty.

This next statement is very controversial, but keep it moving. When things go wrong, don't blame others, take full responsibility for your mistakes. Don't allow others to beat you over the head and hold you hostage to your own misery. Get thee up from that place and move, for the bible says when the leper men made a decision to move, they did it by the thought of simple elimination. If we stay here we will die, because we are hungry, and we have nothing; if we go, they recognized that by moving they would be creating possibilities. So, remember doing nothing never works. Unless you know that God is saying be still and know that I am God. You will know when the Holy Ghost is leading you. Most of the time, as the old saying goes "God is moving by his spirit, signs and wonders in His moving, move oh God, in me."

Keep it moving, if God is for you, who then can be against you? Finish your education, find the opportunity. Create the opportunity. Pray about what to do and how to do it, but go back to school, if that is something you would like to do. Don't depend on your parents to do what you can do for yourself. Your parents don't have to give you the permission to be successful, it would be great to have their blessing, but if by chance they leave you to yourself, be successful. Grab hold to the Lord Jesus, and don't let Him go. Where He goes, I go, and where He leads, I will follow. Oh, this may come by trial and error, but you can do it. You will be front and center, when He call for you. Keep it moving. God is for you, so stop moping, acting like nobody cares. "He cares for you." Put on those things that pertain to life, and make it happen. God has given you power and authority. You can do all things through Christ which strengthen you.

Please don't be sad today because Jesus is watching over you, you can sleep sound and wake, by his touch. Treat your wife right; give her the queenship she deserves. Don't degrade her and put down, she's been faithful to you. He's been faithful to you, stop playing around, you have children, who are depending on you. Give them the best of you.

Do you have everlasting life? The song writer said everything you need is in the house. The house of God. The most important thing you will ever need in this life, is life everlasting and it comes from the Father above. God who made all things. These things were made for His glory and His honor. They are and were created. Look at Isaiah 43:1-7. The

Lord said, "I made you, formed you redeemed you. When you pass through the water, it will not overtake you, when you walk through heated places you will not be burned." Our God is Holy, and anyone who calls on His name and recognize Him as Lord over all the earth shall expect these blessings, so keep it moving.

Isaiah 43 is about movement. It is a special message to encourage the children of God, and their offspring. You will be blessed. You will prosper, and be sustained in Jesus today and forever more. What shall I say to these powerful actions from our Father, who created us for Himself? I'm convinced that because He loves me, and cares for me, I am back in love again.

Introduction:

Book Three: *Sooner or Later*

Happy Birthday Jesus,

Thank you so much for thinking of all humanity, coming down here to this world to bring to us the gift of eternal life, The gift of salvation. I know I didn't deserve it Lord, none of us did, but you did it anyway. You looked upon us all with compassion, and when we see you again, we will see a young man (33) years old, with war wounds that explain your sacrifice without words to follow.

I started my fast a little after 6pm, and to my surprise, two days in - The Lord speaks and says, "Take that number out of your phone. Although He was miles away, The Lord spoke. I listened and almost forgot to do so, before going down to my finished basement to cry out and intercede for others as well as for myself. It was around 6pm, day two. I had been listening to a famous Evangelist, for about three hours via YouTube; I was on fire, purged and humbled.

As I exited my bed, I heard the voice of the Lord ever so sternly, "Take That Number out of Your Phone". I answered and said, "Yes Lord, I didn't mean to forget". I stayed in the basement having a remarkable warfare in the spirit. I felt chains were being broken, and that soul tie was over, and I was in a different place with Father, and I knew it.